THE TRUE "DRAMA OF THE GIFTED CHILD"

The True "Drama of the Gifted Child"

The Phantom Alice Miller—The Real Person

Martin Miller

CONTENTS

SECOND PREFACE FOR THE ENGLISH EDITION OF THE TRUE DRAMA OF THE GIFTED CHILD

My book about the biography of my mother has already been on the market for four years. I have often heard from authors of biographical books how they had finally found serenity, because now their destiny, their whole life experience, had been set down between two book covers, and all their worries were gone.

I did not have this experience – quite the contrary. Shortly after the publication, I was disabused of this notion. I discovered I had opened a Pandora's Box. I had summoned ghosts that I could no longer send back into the bottle—I had to confront them. I had dealt with my biography for decades and knew that my relationship with my parents was very burdensome and painful.

It was only thanks to an impetus from the outside that I wrote the book at all; I myself would never have had the thought. In hindsight I am aware that I was very much afraid to make my experiences with my parents public at all. Writing an honest biography of my mother, revered by her readers as a world-famous author and ideal mother, was particularly hard for me. For I had to describe an Alice Miller

1

who never appeared this way in her books. I had great feelings of guilt about betraying my mother. For me, writing the book was never a matter of accusation or revenge, but one of justice. All readers envied me my good and compassionate mother. Initially, I was very confused, and then shocked at how my mother portrayed herself in public. Time and again she asked me never to make anything of her private life public. But I came to the conclusion that I had to publish the truth, primarily for my own sake. However, I was confronted in the first place with the difficulty of discovering the truth about my parents.

Over the course of my inquiries during the last four years, I found out that my parents had constructed for me a grandiose lie.

Thus the following dynamic developed between myself and my parents: The more my parents were afraid that I would see through their lies, the more they became violent towards me. By all available means they tried to intimidate me. My book reveals the arduous path by which I nevertheless defied parental violence and ultimately uncovered the lie.

Especially in this day and age, courage and honesty are needed to uncover lies. Soon, though, the sustained lie topples over into a fear of discovery, and fear of the truth. The lie is defended by all available means against the truth, and violence becomes common practice.

My own work on myself has strengthened my conviction as a psychotherapist about the importance of processing clients' biographies with them. My own experience helped me work through these biographies as honestly as possible. The aim is not to single out culprits, but is to give clients the right to feel, and finally to be able to articulate their subjective biographical experience. I give people the room that they need to become aware of their past as a lived experience. Finally they sit across from someone who takes their experiences seriously and is not afraid to confront himself with the fate of the other.

The book that I have written is an example of what such an experience might look like. I also want to give courage to people to face their history. Such a confrontation with one's past is also active peace work because I no longer need to unconsciously pass my repressed biographical experience onto others. As an adult shaped by my childhood experiences, I was still vulnerable to letting myself be manipulated into a life-threatening situation—a traumatic experience that haunted me for years and that I could free myself from only with great effort.

This is why for me today the following rule applies: When I process how I was victimized as a child, and other traumatic experiences, I no longer need to victimize others by identifying with the perpetrator.

Martin Miller
March 2018

LETTER OF MY MOTHER OF
NOVEMBER 22, 1987

St. Remy, November 22, 1987

*D*ear Martin,
         I have needed thirty years to find out that I lived for such a long time and had two children with a man who did not once listen to me during all those years + who never saw me for who I am. At the last minute, I was able to save myself from final self-destruction + fortunately also Julika. I could not save you; I tried: I offered to pay for you a course of therapy that has helped me see realities after I had avoided and been blind to them for sixty years. You refused my offer with big gestures and did not want to hear anything about it. Instead, you are beginning to imitate more and more your father's behavior, obviously without noticing it, because you deny it fiercely when I confront you with it.

Why did I need thirty years to open my eyes? Why did I need sixty years to see how cruel, destructive, exploitative, thoroughly mendacious and loveless my mother was? That she systematically destroyed love and life within me, and later did the same with my sister and my nephew?

         Because the repression of the pain of childhood is so incredibly strong + because I had to learn, in order to maintain it, not to be aware, not to feel anything + to believe the false assurances that she would "love" me. I also had to acquire very early on the desire to understand others and to be helpful, whereas only disgust would have been the sole appropriate reaction: disgust and flight towards other humans more capable of loving. But my fate did not grant me this possibility. There was no escape for me; in the end, I even became my mother's savior, and when I thought after the war that I could withdraw from her at long last, I fled to a human being who treated me in similar ways like she had done, and who I, once again, wanted to save and to deliver to life so that he would allow me and my children to live.

But one cannot help the other when he cannot question himself at all and needs to feel grandiose. Also, one cannot change the other, only solely and exclusively oneself. And only if one really wants it.

I had this will, because I must have sensed, despite my blindness, that not all humans are as destructive as my mother and that it is criminal to build up one's own power at the expense of one's children. Now I say that I _sensed_ it, because I did not want to become like my mother since forever, under any circumstances. Any, even the slightest similarity drove me to despair when I recognized it, and I did not rest until I could dissolve it by clarification with the other—something which my mother never did. But basically, I did not know _why_ I did not want to identify myself with her. I was afraid of this knowledge. In the past, I never would have been allowed to think or say: my mother was a cruel human being, she destroyed the lives of her two children without any trace of a guilty conscience, while she believed herself to be loving and caring. But I carried this truth inside, I sensed it and all during my life looked for ways that might have helped me to lift the repression.

I looked in vain. In philosophy and psychoanalysis. Thanks to writing and painting, the truth at first acquired vague outlines, *and finally, I succeeded, in my therapy, to discover the whole truth about my childhood.*

Among the many people who write to me, there are always individuals who absolutely <u>want to know</u> what once happened to them, and very many, who under no circumstances wish to know, who have come to terms with the repression of their truth, be it through destructive behavior at the expense of others, be it through self-destruction by addiction. Very often, all three kinds of defenses can be found in the same person.

When you were here in June, the hope came alive in me that you want to find the strength and the will to live your feelings, to find your history, to trace your childhood suffering, to recognize it, and to eventually free yourself from your destructive and self-destructive patterns before you yourself have children and start a family. It seemed to me that your heart could open itself here, in this landscape, and you might allow little Martin to live. During your last visit, I could no longer preserve this hope. It seems that you are not able, or not yet able, to perceive what really had happened to you. That is why you are in danger to let others suffer for your blindness, and to consider this quite right and normal.

After a break of several months, you begin again to show me the all-too-familiar patterns: to wreak your rage on me and this all the more, and more uninhibited, the friendlier and more cordially I meet you. And every attempt at clarifying bounces off your shouting—which protects you from listening.

Your cells have stored this behavior early, but you have obviously not seen through its evilness, otherwise you would not be so clueless when you are confronted with it: like it now happens to my cordiality with you, in the same way your filial cordiality was once answered with beatings. That these beatings came along with assurances of love and "caring for you" made the confusion even bigger. Because you believed these assurances! Like every child, you had to forget with the fried sausage how the beatings had hurt. But your

7

brain has linked and stored one with the other: the beatings and the fried sausage (or chocolate, or chocolate cream cake). And in your behavior towards me, you let me experience both, as if I were little Martin and you the big boss, who distributes on a whim alternately "love" or beatings on me and wishes to remain clueless.

You can only afford this behavior with me because I represent the child, don't wield power, don't blackmail you, don't scare you into panic, and am ready, again and again, for a conversation with you. I stand by my position, but I cannot and will not accept the role of victim. No longer will I allow myself to be tormented or seduced, not even by my own son, particularly as I know that it would not benefit him at all. As long as you find victims, little Martin remains imprisoned and numb, and you think you can demonstrate and fool the other, something that no one will accept from you in the long run. For the emptiness is noticed all too clearly, when the child within is strangled for good. I have experienced this sufficiently. Even the "greatest" roles are nothing but facades + remain miserable, if not ridiculous.

Sometimes you treat me with such a palpable hatred, as if I had once been your persecutor. But this I was <u>not</u>. For sure, I did not meet your needs for security and protection, could not give you much of what you needed, and have suffered myself from this inability. Today I can see that, as an unloved child, I was incapable of giving you enough love. But this did not absolve me from the responsibility, which I took on when I wanted to have a child.

You once told me that your father always used to beat you in my absence. I should have guessed and sensed this and never should have negligently handed you over, all alone, to this power. And if I myself had once been a protected child, my antennas would have warned me! Because I had indeed seen enough of what was going on in my <u>presence</u>. Therefore I <u>should have</u> protected you absolutely from your father's blows. That I had too little courage to see and bear the truth does not lessen my <u>actual guilt</u> towards you. Thus I would *accept the reproach that I stood by as I abandoned you to abuse, because this reproach is valid and justified. You can also make all other reproaches against me, which are justified, and check them. I would never refuse to answer you.*

But I refuse to be the outlet for the suppressed rage, which his blows have caused in you. And I refuse to be the child that you hit on the head, for whatever reasons you have to do it. Because I was not your persecutor.

It is very sad for me that all my attempts to get into a conversation with you here, and to clarify facts, bounced off a thick wall. But that could be ranked somehow as a defense of my reproaches. Because, after all, I <u>did</u> blame you; I stand by that.

But much sadder was for me the observation that you sometimes snapped at me out of the blue, without my giving you even the slightest provocation. I did not have the feeling that you treated me like your father had treated me, but that you abused me in the same way he had handled <u>you</u>. Then I felt, for a moment, like a completely trampled down child, which I myself had never been with him; but I was able to observe how he handled you.

It has frightened me and given me much food for thought that you don't seem to notice your newly acquired and therefore reversible automatisms (one would think: not at all), that you seem to consider your present behavior as perfectly normal (and thereby are justifying his), and that you show no interest to change anything about it. Have you ever asked yourself, which price you are paying for your repression?

It is a tragic fate to have a father who beats a helpless child. That is not your fault. But not wanting to see, as an adult, how he is, and to sacrifice one's developmental opportunities and maturation chances for this blindness, to turn oneself slowly into this father, in order to protect him and to spare him—this is not fate. This need not to be so. It is rather a destructive and self-destructive decision, for which you as an adult bear the entire responsibility.

❧ ❧ ❧

I wanted to put this letter into my testament in order to avoid your lack of understanding, because I know how you react to the faintest reference to your father. You close your ears and think: "Those two should fight each other without me." Because from both sides, you hear nothing but evil about the other. But no matter how much this comparison and this equalization might add up for an unsuspecting stranger, for me it is utterly misleading. Because for a long time now, I have not had any need to retaliate against this man. But I <u>do have</u> a need, and this much more strongly the more I can see, to protect my children.

This is why I decided to send you this letter <u>now</u>. If at all possible, I want to save your children from also having to suffer because of the curse of your and my childhood. This can only be avoided when you one day wake up from your sleep + begin to see the realities within + around you.

This is a heartfelt wish for you from your mother

I. PREFACE

When I had the opportunity, several weeks after my mother's death in 2010, to give an interview to the news magazine *Der Spiegel*, the following exchange took place between myself and interviewers Elke Schmitter and Phillipp Oehmke, and their questions haunted me until the writing of this book:

Q. You say your mother based a life's work on finding ways to uncover traumas in other people, yet could not find a path to discuss her own traumas with her son?

A. I made countless attempts to talk about this with her. Just like you are doing now with me. But I was biting on granite. I am not able to help you further. I am not only her son, I am also a therapist, hence someone who studies and deals with biographies, but I did not get through to her. At some point, one accepts it. My mother's stonewalling made it impossible for me to get closer to her during the last thirty years. I had to acquiesce.

Q. Your mother created a unique body of work which says: psychoanalysis cannot help the traumatized individual, but there is another, independent path to resolve the repressions of childhood and to come alive again—and I, Alice Miller, will try to show you this path. Now we find, after ten minutes of conversation with you, that in her body of work your mother did not even touch on one important aspect of her own biography. In other words, she could not apply her own set of tools to the greatest trauma of her life.

A. Yes, even though she saw so many things accurately in her books. It is my personal tragedy that I, a child of the war generation, did not manage to establish an emotional relationship with my parents.

Q. Help us: Is not lack of relationship exactly what your mother marked as parental cruelty and a cause of psychological damage? (*Der Spiegel*, 18/2010)

At that time, it would not have occurred to me in my wildest dreams to write a book about my mother. She was too alien for me as a describable person. Only after I met an American publisher of her books, at the Frankfurt book fair in the fall of 2010, did I begin to think about it seriously. The publisher impressed upon me that it might be of tremendous benefit to myself and my mother's readers to write a book about her. This conversation worked in me and triggered contradictory feelings. Initially, I rebelled against the idea, and considered the prospect of writing a book about my mother as absurd. But despite the immense emotional resistance, the idea would not let go of me, and I decided, reluctantly, to tackle this difficult project.

There was an initial problem—I knew far too little about my mother: Alice Miller—in this book I will often refer to my mother in the third person—kept the story of her life tightly wrapped, and made her private life a well-guarded secret. She was particularly secretive about the years during the war. My mother had, this much is known, survived World War II as a Jewess in Poland. But she never talked about this time, except in camouflage, or dressed in literary disguise. She said virtually nothing to me about this time in her life; only when I was forty-one years old did I learn scant details. During my childhood and youth, everything Jewish, and also everything Polish, was kept from me. I never learned the Polish language, my parents' mother tongue, nor was I taught anything about Jewish culture. I grew up as an artificial cultural product, and was raised Swiss, a citizen of a country foreign to my parents. As is typical for survivors, I represented the so-called fresh start after survival. That is one side of it.

To the extent that my mother's never-articulated misery was hidden from me, I was still just as strongly affected by it—this is clear to me today after the investigations conducted for this book. We know from studies about children of Holocaust survivors that they are very much monopolized by their parents. They have to represent the emotional counterpart that was missing during the bad time. These children become their parents' crutch and means of existence. This process, the reversal of the parent-child relationship, is called *parentification*. Parents, plagued by traumatic intrusions, fall back on the emotional support of their children. As my mother described it superbly in her first book, *The Drama of the Gifted Child*, children have an extraordinary talent to grasp parental needs in an ingeniously nonverbal way. They understand perfectly what is expected of them, and behave accordingly. I did the same.

The relationship with my mother—this is how I can finally understand it today—had all the characteristics of such a twisted bond. Added to this was the transfer of the repressed persecution traumatization. In other words, my mother and I were very close in a neurotic way, had a strong bond through possessive closeness. In this way, I became emotionally a part of my mother's Holocaust experience—of course without knowing it—as a child and as an adult. I became a witness to, even part of the war trauma, without knowing what really had happened. I became a participant in a history of suffering, even though—or precisely because—it was unknown to me. Flying blindly, I experienced the persecution of my mother by the Nazis, and the consequences of this persecution.

Henryk Broder (born 1946), the German author and publicist, describes in Erwin Leiser's 1982 film *Life After Survival* his fate as a child of parents who survived the Holocaust, in the following way: "I had the perpetual feeling as if I were restrained in a coordinate system of horror that was unknown and invisible to me, but which severely burdened me, that I cannot defend myself against." I recognize myself in these sentences.

I remember visiting relatives in Zurich and seeing objects in their apartment that were strange to me. Magically, the wooden figures on the sideboard, which represented orthodox Jewish men, attracted me. A Hanukkah candelabra also stood there. But I never dared to ask someone what it all might mean. The unspoken prohibition "don't ask" worked completely. Again and again, even as an adult, I was confronted with my mother's fear that anything of her private life might be revealed. Until her death, she meticulously made sure that nothing personal got out to the public.

Only the aforementioned *Spiegel* interview, and the suggestion of the American publisher, shook me out of my blind obedience to my mother.

Despite my guilt feelings, I sensed there was much more at stake than mere misgivings over whether it was the right thing to do to continue withholding my mother' life history from her readers. The point for me was rather if I would finally dare to explore my own history, if I could dare to discover my biographical roots.

I am well familiar with my mother's books. In *Breaking Down the Walls of Silence* (1990), Alice Miller recommends to all her readers to uncover their truth, their history, and to dismantle repressions. Now I recognized, despite years of my own therapy and decades of experience in my work as a therapist, that for such a project I had to overcome not only a wall of silence, but also a huge wall of guilt feelings.

In this emotional state I made a first attempt at writing this book. As I was writing, long forgotten memories came up, and I believed indeed that I was describing my mother's life. Not until the discussions with my editor Evamaria Bohle did I realize that I was caught in a confusion of roles, that I was mainly depicting my emotional experience with my mother, and that "the facts" were saturated by the judgments that my mother had passed on to me.

I started all over, visited contemporary witnesses, still-living relatives of my mother—her cousins Irenka and Ala in the United States. A wondrous and hitherto unknown world began to reveal itself to me, the prewar world in which my mother had grown up, and which was brutally annihilated by World War II and the Nazi persecution of the Jews. Today I am convinced that Alice Miller's inability to be a loving mother is due to the firmly encapsulated trauma of the years of persecution from 1939 until 1945. By now, I am astonished how my mother managed to write so objectively in her book *For Your Own Good* (1980) about the childhood of Adolf Hitler. It strikes me as particularly absurd how my mother was continually reproached, in the public eye and in published criticism of her book, for trivializing Hitler's actions. You cannot hide and repress your own history better than that.

THE DEMOLITION OF THE WALL OF SILENCE, A COMPLEX ENDEAVOR

The problems of factually researching this book were intermingled with immense guilt feelings. By writing this book, I committed a transgression of boundaries, I broke a taboo, I overstepped a line which I had always been forbidden to cross. How much my mother had been at pains to keep her life story under lock and key, and how ruthless she could become when someone was on the trail of her secrets, is shown by the experience of the American writer and psychoanalyst Jeffrey Masson. On the internet, Masson commented on a 2010 article by Daphne Merkin entitled: "Private Drama. Alice Miller was an authority on childhood trauma, but she stayed mum about her own." Masson wrote:

Very interesting article! (...) One small correction: I did not "suspect" she was Jewish; she told me she was Jewish. She talked about it in great detail with my then wife, Therese Claire Masson, who was also Jewish, and also from Warsaw (she was a child in the Warsaw Ghetto). Although they spoke in Polish most of the time, I sometimes joined the conversation, as I have always been fascinated (obsessed others would say) with the Holocaust. When Alice Miller asked me to do an interview with her for a European publication I gladly agreed, and all went well until I asked about her life in Warsaw and how this may have had an impact on her views. After all, I claimed then, and still do, that any analyst who ignores the trauma that is the Holocaust, is shirking his or her duty. Surely trauma lies at the very heart of Freud's psychoanalysis. She blew up, and began to cry. How could I join the long list of people who had abused her? I had no idea what she meant, and she would not explain, but from that moment our friendship suffered and never recovered. I still feel puzzled, because I know she agreed with me about the importance of trauma, and in fact had come to Berkeley to spend a week with me talking about it before I wrote my book, *The Assault on Truth*.

This behavior is in my experience typical for my mother. Only with Ala, Esther, and Irenka, the cousins who had also survived the war, did she have an emotionally close bond. Otherwise, her relationships were invariably marked by a burdensome tension; the reason was, in my view, that my mother had to keep everything under control. When relationships got too intimate, when a partner made "demands" or came too close, then the relationship turned into a fight, and war prevailed. You could be close to her, a friend, and then suddenly you were branded a dangerous enemy.

My relationship with my mother also suffered from this ambivalence. Since the eighties, when I established myself as a psychotherapist, and my mother became famous as an author of books, our relationship steadily changed for the worse, and took on a highly neurotic quality. During the development of her first three books, I remained my mother's close confidant, but the more I struck out on my own, the more our relationship deteriorated. Then followed decades of dreadful conflicts, gross emotional infringements—I will address this later—which prompted me to withdraw further and further. Eventually, she began to treat me like an enemy. She effectively made me feel like a monster she wanted to destroy. Today I am sure that also in this regard the denial of her war trauma began to have a destructive impact. I will come back to this later, too. As a therapist, I knew how to set boundaries, but as a son, her tantrums hurt me deeply. This will also be the point of this book, and my emotional scars did not make writing it any easier.

Nevertheless—and this is very important to me—I do not see this book as yet another offering in the series of reckonings in which children of prominent personalities judge their deceased parents harshly. Nor do I intend to suggest that my mother's behavior toward me negates the merits of her books and the importance of her theories. Her books, and her paintings as well, were developed in a wide, creative space where Alice Miller could be herself, free from her grievances. Unfortunately, she had to split off this space from her real existence. To be sure, her books were a great success, and in them many readers saw themselves understood, and above all felt accepted in their emotional suffering. However, the books were worlds apart from the real life of Alice Miller and the way she treated her son. It was not a good experience to be the son of Alice Miller—quite the contrary. And yet, my mother was a great researcher on childhood.

In this book, I try to connect these disparate worlds of Alice Miller. That is why it is so important for me to describe my relationship with my mother in greater detail than I would otherwise prefer. Dissociation was obviously my mother's only option to attain some quality of life for herself after the war. And indeed, I can see in my mother's fight for her quality of life an encouraging example for many people not to give in, no matter what life has dealt them. On the other hand, my mother also exemplifies, in a terrifying way, what can happen when severe trauma—caused by war, persecution, and other violent experiences—is not processed. For this reason, I am also grateful that the trauma therapist Oliver Schubbe, who in 2000 worked with my mother, agreed to write an afterword for this book.

A word, too, about my role: during the writing process, I have noticed that the most difficult task for me consists of not letting facts, on the one hand, and memories (mine and Alice Miller's), on the other hand, merge with one another, and with the explanations I offer. I may have fallen short of accomplishing this. Nevertheless I hope that the picture I draw of my mother will do justice to her realities. In the true drama of the gifted child, it shall be possible to get closer to Alice Miller as a human being.

Martin Miller

II. THE END—NO GRAVE FOR ALICE MILLER

My mother lived out her final years in the French commune of Saint-Rémy-de-Provence, and, on April 14, 2010, chose to die there, but no one visiting the Saint-Rémy cemetery will find her burial plot. Nor is there a grave for Alice Miller in Zurich, Switzerland, where she resided from 1946 until 1985, and where she began her career as a world-famous researcher on childhood. She did not want a grave. My mother was cremated, and her ashes were scattered near the small mountain lake outside Saint-Rémy, where she often sat by the shore and recited her texts into a Dictaphone.

I had virtually no contact with my mother since the end of the nineties, and was not even aware that she had given up her residence in Switzerland. She told me about her move to France only a short time before her death. My mother evidently saw the need to barricade herself in France during the last years of her life; her sole conduit to the world was the internet. In Saint-Rémy, it appears she had little social interaction apart from a woman friend and the woman's family, who assisted her greatly in all practical matters of life. It was not until after my mother's death that I realized how closely she had bound herself to that family. Following my mother's estate distribution, my relationship with her friend became increasingly strained and filled with suspicion. Today, all communication with the friend has been broken off.

I reestablished contact with my mother by email in the year before her death, prompted by her own comments on her web page. I was offended by some of her sweeping statements about therapists. She could not think of a single practitioner worthy of her recommendation. At the same time, she named criteria that inform my own code as a psychotherapist. I felt affronted, and could not let her remarks go unchallenged.

At first, my mother reacted uncertainly, and she called me a short time later to ask me not to attack her any more. She could no longer bear such arguments. I gave in and did not comment any further on our burdened relationship. I had to accept that it was too late to resolve our dispute via conversation.

By early 2010, my mother, at 87, suddenly became severely ill. She lost weight rapidly, but refused medical treatment. Initially, she was not interested in a diagnosis. Not until her pain had reached intolerable proportions did she contact me again. In light of our problematic relationship I decided to forgo a visit to Provence, and she did not object. Up until the day she died, our only direct contact was by telephone.

Above all, my mother voiced the wish for assisted dying. Because of the unbearable pain, she had finally visited a doctor, who diagnosed her with advanced-stage pancreatic cancer. Only morphine made the pain somewhat bearable. She did not want to live any more, wanted to take her death into her own hands and to avoid, at all costs, any dependence on others. She asked for my active support in this undertaking, and was displeased, to say the least, when I pointed out that even in Switzerland assisted dying was no easy matter. Though she accepted my objections, she could not be dissuaded, and began to look for alternatives to implement her plan for assisted dying. And so she organized her death without my help.

I will never forget how, on the morning of April 14, my mother telephoned to say goodbye forever. It was a short conversation, in which she wished me "all the best for the future." An absurd situation. She had planned everything with military precision, and when I finally arrived in Saint-Rémy, her remains had already been cremated.

These are of course very personal decisions, how one's remains shall be disposed of, and how to shape one's death, if one can shape it at all. But with all due respect for my mother's wishes, I find it tragic to consider that even in death—indeed, even beyond death—she tried to stay in control. Now, more than three years later, I know much more about my mother than I ever knew while she was alive. And today, it seems to me that at the very end of her life, amid all her pain and suffering, she was still saying triumphantly: "You won't get me!" And perhaps it is true, that in the end she succeeded in escaping for good. She shook off all her pursuers—the demons that, as a Holocaust survivor, haunted her all her life, and even those that might still come forward, the new Nazis who would not shy away from the desecration of graves. What a tragic victory.

III. Inherited Identity— The Jewess

WHAT MY MOTHER
RECOUNTED: THE PAIN OF
CHILDHOOD

We had relatives in Zurich: Ala, my mother's favorite aunt; her husband Bunio; and their daughter Irenka. In their apartment, there were these aforementioned objects, which attracted me magically as a child. They stood on the sideboard: wooden figures that represented orthodox Jewish men, and a Hanukkah candelabra. That my maternal relatives were Jewish, and what this meant for my family—these were not subjects of discussion in the Miller household.

It would be a mistake, however, to think that my mother never discussed with me her childhood in a strictly religious Jewish family. But she did so in a manner which made it impossible for me to form an emotional connection with my own Jewish heritage, or with my relatives and ancestors. They remained strangers. My mother stressed entirely different matters in her account of her Jewish upbringing. She portrayed Judaism as an authoritarian religion, and her parents as stupid, mentally dull people, who against better judgment held on to all sorts of meaningless rules and laws.

She recounted how she, as a little girl, already quarreled constantly with her father, and especially with her mother, over their observance of Jewish laws. These rules struck her as nonsense that defied rational explanation. She could talk herself into a rage, and rant about what she perceived as the hypocritical behavior of her parents—her father, for example, believed he was exempt from the alleged all-important dietary laws because of health reasons. What impressed me above all was the excessive rage my mother carried inside, the origins of which I could not quite explain to myself, but which accompanied all her memories of her parents and her family. In any event, I never sensed that my mother had any intimate connection with Jewish culture, even after the start of the 1980s, when she began to concern herself more with her heritage. In her eyes, the Jewish culture she had experienced as a child remained a prison. Sweepingly, she portrayed the social environment of her childhood as an obstinate, obedient, unthinking social group, which complied unfeelingly and uncritically with all requirements, and regarded the mandatory laws as the guiding principle of conduct. She talked about her family in a way that made clear that she had set herself apart as different, as not belonging. I experienced the taste of her memories as full of embitterment and rage.

All of this confused me lastingly. I was not only left unacquainted with my Jewish roots, but even more inexplicably, my mother, who as I well knew had survived the Holocaust, unceasingly berated Judaism. She denounced without restraint Jewish customs which, in her view, were absurd. Increasingly, I got the feeling that my mother's condemnation of Judaism was a sacrilege. Was she not scorning the victims of persecution? I was ashamed of her, but I never addressed my questions. Until her death, this subject was taboo, and it remained so with my relatives. I did not raise the issue, and nobody raised it with me. The wall of silence was insurmountable.

Basically, it was not until I made the decision to write this book that I took a different path and broke the taboo. I began to do research, and visited the United States, where I talked to the last survivors of this generation of my family. With their help, I have tried to reconstruct my mother's family history, *my own* family history. It was appalling for me to discover this hidden, rich world, and harrowing to realize to what extent my mother had disowned her origins. And as my mother's disavowal of her past became distressingly clear to me, I was shocked on another level by what I already knew: that between 1933 and 1945, the culture of my mother's childhood was nearly obliterated. It was as if an emotional door was opening within me: no longer did I only know that my mother was a Holocaust victim, but feelings began to awaken in me. Her lifelong silence developed frightening, indescribably painful contours.

WHAT I FOUND OUT:
ALICIJA ENGLARD AND HER
FAMILY UNTIL 1939

My mother was born in the Polish town Piotrków Trybunalski in the Lodz province (36 kilometers south of Lodz and 154 kilometers away from Warsaw) to an orthodox Jewish family. Since its incorporation in the Middle Ages, Piotrków had had a large Jewish community; between the end of the 1920s and the beginning of World War II, it was home to roughly twenty-five thousand Jews, both Orthodox and liberal. The latter regarded religion as a private matter, and identified with the way of life of the nation in which they lived.

Alicija grew up in a large Jewish family. Three generations lived under one roof. Her grandfather was named Abraham Dov Englard. He had come to Piotrków at the beginning of the 20th century. With his wife Sarah he founded a household goods store and thereby achieved considerable prosperity. He could afford to buy a three-story house in the middle of the township of Piotrków, near the train station. The Englards also owned the first telephone in town, with the phone number 1.

Abraham was a Hasidic Jew. Aside from his work, he occupied himself primarily with religious subjects, and studied the Talmud and Torah. In his community he was considered a wise man who could dispense advice on religious questions. He also actively tended to the poor and was eminently respected. He was praised for his intelligence, his charisma, and his humor. He must have had a winning and above all gracious radiance. Although he made no exception for himself in keeping with the religious rules, he had an open heart for those less compliant. Because of an eye condition, which vexed him from his early years and led to blindness in old age, he traveled across half of Europe, accompanied by his wife, and sought medical attention. Thus, he was not a narrow-minded provincial, but an educated, well-traveled man. As he delved more and more into religious studies, his wife Sarah managed the business. Abraham and Sarah Englard had five children, two sons and three daughters: Fishel, Meylech—my mother's father—Dora, Frania, and Ala.

Her family, the aunts and uncles of my mother, reflected the multifaceted lives of Jews during this time. Fishel, the eldest son, for instance, went his own way. He was enthusiastic about Zionism and seems to have been in general a nonconformist. He had an illegitimate daughter, Eva. Together with her, he immigrated to Palestine at the end of the 1920s, and participated in the fight of the Zionists for the state of Israel. Later, after the war, he worked in a kibbutz; Eva also remained in the newly founded state of Israel.

Meylech, my grandfather, was the second son. He was regarded as frail and needy. My mother's cousin characterized him in the following way:

Meylech was very reserved and his demeanor was unassuming, he seemed passive and inconspicuous.

He was very religious, like his father, but was always overshadowed by him. He was the most obedient of all of Abraham's children. He did not have professional training, he helped out in his father's business. According to custom, his father also chose his wife. Although he was in love with another woman, Meylech complied with his father's wish. He simply did not dare to rebel against parental authority. He would and could not assert himself. Even though he suffered from the paternalism of his parents, he remained silent and resigned himself to his fate.

Meylech's wife, my grandmother, was called Gutta. She came from Kielce, a neighboring village of Piotrków, and from a simple family. "Gutta," according to my mother's cousin, "was very ambitious."

She was cold and unfeeling. Time and again, she had to urge her husband on. Meylech and Gutta did not have an emotional relationship with each other. They remained strangers to each other. It was simply an arranged, prescribed relationship, which was agony for both of them. Even though one accepted the verdict, internally one rebelled against it. Gutta made every effort to be accepted by the family, but she did not succeed. She was not very intelligent, and poorly educated.

After the two sons, Fishel and Meylech, three daughters were born: Dora, Franja, and Ala. Dora was married off to a doctor in Warsaw and moved to the capital. She gave birth to a son there, and with her family she led a life as a liberal Jew until the war started. The entire family died in the Warsaw Ghetto.

Franja was married off as a young woman to a rich businessman in Berlin. His name was Jarkor Mendelssohn. His father, himself a highly successful businessman, had imported wood from Russia to Europe. When World War I began, and trading ended, the young couple moved to Copenhagen. There, Ala, the first child of the family, was born; she lives in America today. At the beginning of the 1920s, the family returned to Berlin, and Ala's father began to build a new business. Jarkor Mendelssohn specialized in real estate, founded a mortgage bank, and bought and managed properties. In Berlin, two more children came into the world: Esther and Marcel. The Mendelssohn family was liberal-minded and led a luxurious life style.

The youngest daughter of my great-grandparents was Ala. She was the baby of the family and enjoyed many freedoms. In contrast to her siblings she was permitted to attend a public school in Piotrków. Ala moved back and forth between the devout and the secular world. In this manner she met her future husband, Bunio Zussman. He was several years older and, coming from an Orthodox parental home, opted for a liberal lifestyle. Ala married Bunio—it was a love match—and they socialized mainly in the liberal upper middle-class of Polish-Jewish society. This particular community was rife with academics—doctors, lawyers and artists. The representatives of this society identified themselves mainly as Poles, and their everyday language was not Yiddish but Polish.

The five children of Abraham Englard, the aunts and uncles of Alicija, show how diverse the social environment of my mother's childhood really was. Fishel represented the combative, Jewish-national idea of Zionism; Franja lived among the wealthy bourgeoisie of Berlin; Meylech, Alicija's father, continued in the Orthodox tradition; Dora married into the middle class; and Ala lived in the liberal, intellectual Polish-Jewish society. All members of the family were prosperous, and did not lack material comfort. They owned houses large enough for extended families, and could afford servants. Even if individual family members held different cultural views, the presence of grandfather Abraham Englard kept the family cohesively bound together.

Into this milieu, Alicija was born on January 12, 1923 as the eldest daughter of Gutta and Meylech Englard. Her sister Irena came into the world five years later. The women who were my conversational partners agreed that Alicija was an unusual and a so-called difficult child. Her cousin Irenka Taurek, the daughter of Ala and Bunio Zussman, describes her as follows:

Your mother was a very bright child. But she was not very social. She always withdrew and spent most of her time reading. She often behaved very arrogantly towards others and showed everyone how superior she felt. She was very critical and observed carefully what others did. She continually asked questions and left no one in peace. From an early age, she always asserted her will. She was very persistent and could not be argued out of an idea she had set her mind on. Very early she expressed her critical view of Orthodox Judaism, and she got her own way that she, like her aunt Ala, was allowed to attend a Polish public school. Her sister had to attend a Jewish school.

From early on, Alicija believed that she would learn too little in a Jewish school and that it would be very boring there. But unlike her aunt Ala, who opened herself socially in the public school and had Polish girlfriends, Alicija always remained very reserved and avoided friendships that were too close. Also in school she remained a loner. Everyone noticed how suspicious she was and that she believed others were hostile towards her. Her arrogant manner was certainly also a protection to keep people at a distance. Alicija had rather a good childhood, as she always got what she wanted. Everybody gave in because they wanted to be left alone.

She was especially often—already before I was born—at our home with my parents. Ala and Bunio lived in the big house of his parents. They were also Orthodox, but in their attitude much more tolerant. My parents lived as assimilated Jews in a very liberal way, and Alicija was magically attracted by this world. My mother said that she felt much more comfortable in our home than with her parents. She often argued with her parents, in our home she could recharge her batteries.

Anyhow, she rejected the Orthodox Jewish world more and more vehemently. I think that she was ashamed of her own parents. Her father was not only deeply pious, he also was a weak man and had little professional success. He remained financially dependent on his father and did not manage to stand on his own feet. Alicija experienced her mother as strict and ambitious. Also her relationship with her sister Irena was very bad. Irena was an alive, open child, who liked to play and did not want to busy herself with books. She enjoyed life and did not take it all so seriously. This did not suit Alicija at all, and she despised her sister. This sibling constellation did not change until the death of Alicija. Even though the sisters tried to reconcile in an exchange of letters towards the end of their lives, they did not succeed. Particularly Alicija hindered an amicable relationship again and again. Even surviving the war together could not change anything about this negative relationship.

From 1931 until the Nazis' seizure of power, Alicija lived with her family with the Mendelssohns in Berlin. Abraham Englard had asked his daughter Franja to help out her brother Meylech and to get a job for him with her husband. Alicija loved life in Berlin. From a prosperous home she arrived in an environment of wealth. Her older cousin Ala, the eldest daughter of Franja, remembers:

> Then, I was already fifteen years old and your mother only nine. But I always had the feeling of socializing with her on an equal footing. She was so intelligent. When she came to Berlin, she did not speak a word of German. After two months, she had an almost perfect command of the language. Alicija felt very comfortable in Berlin and we enjoyed the summer months in our house at the Wannsee.
>
> When Hitler came into power, my father had to leave Berlin and fled to Paris. We children and our mother returned to Poland. We lived near Warsaw. Alicija moved with her family back to Piotrków. I think it was very hard for her to leave Berlin. If Hitler had not come to power, she certainly would have never returned with her family to Poland.

After a year, Aunt Franja returned with her children to Berlin and tried to save what could be saved. She sold banks and houses, and moved with her children to join her husband Jarkor in Paris. When the Germans were outside of Paris, the family fled in their motorcar to Spain and Portugal, where they remained for some time. When the Germans approached the Spanish border, they moved on to

America. Ala and her sister Esther remained there; after the war, brother Marcel moved with his parents back to Paris, and today lives in Israel.

Back in Piotrków, ten-year-old Alicija again attended the Polish school and had to adjust to everyday life and the problems of a Jewish girl who did not want to be Jewish. This arrangement lasted for six years—until the war ripped her life completely apart.

THE TRUE SELF AND THE
SUBJECTIVE WORLD

Interestingly, the idea never occurred to any of the relatives I talked to that my mother might have suffered in her childhood. In their eyes, she had—until the beginning of the war—a good, indeed, even an ideal childhood. She was spoiled, she often got her way, she got everything she wanted. She did not suffer material limitations, could read and dedicate herself to her education. There was even a household staff, so she was spared even the need to perform any housework.

The conflicts with her parents regarding religion were certainly known, but were not perceived as having existential importance. Perhaps her uncles and aunts, who, unlike Meylech, had almost all chosen the liberal path, might even have found the protestations of Meylech's eldest daughter a source of amusement.

In contrast to this perception, over the course of her life, my mother became increasingly vehement in her accusations against her parents. Towards the end of her life, she virtually assailed her remaining relatives to confirm how badly her parents had treated her. I was absent from this phase of her life, we did not have contact during this time, but I consider it plausible in light of my experiences with her.

So, how does one reconcile these different points of view regarding my mother? One can affirm, I think, that my mother must have been an attentive and very sensitive child. Her rage was justified and a consequence of the unempathetic behavior within her social environment. Though her adult relatives may have thought otherwise, she experienced firsthand that her questions, her criticisms, were interpreted and punished as disobedient behavior. Neither father nor mother, nor her little sister, who obviously interacted in less conflicting ways with her parents, understood the angry girl. She had no allies, except maybe her aunt Ala and Ala's husband Bunio, with whom she spent a lot of time. But she felt nevertheless that she was at the mercy of the mother's castigations, and saw her father as weak and unreasonable, and her little sister as a conformist rival. She reacted by withdrawing: her relatives told me that young Alicija was a solitary person. She retreated into her room and read her beloved books. She had no girlfriends and never wanted to play with other children. She was described as arrogant. In addition, she was mistrustful of other people, which further justified her withdrawal from her social group.

In the terminology of her own theories: she painfully experienced that as a child, one stands as a rule all alone, if one wants to live one's own true self in defiance of the family's values. Alicija did not have the right to her own opinion, she was censored and indoctrinated. From these experiences, a subjective realization strengthened in the little girl, which in her adult life led, among other things, inexorably to her thesis that Judaism as a whole was a persecuting, repressive, and misanthropic ideology. This religion and this culture—embodied for the child above all in her parents—became for her a daily fight for survival.

Every human being develops in such a situation a subjective, inner world, which significantly defines her future actions. These impressions are so strong that also new experiences are mostly integrated into an existing structure. In so doing, they do not necessarily alter the structure, but instead reinforce the subjective world and the perceptions resulting from it. As my mother's depicted her childhood experiences, the threat was not the outer existential danger for Jews in a hostile environment, but the repressive constraints imposed by the religious laws within the family. Alicija felt neglected by her own family, not by the social environment. This inner psychic coordinate system later became the basis of her psychological theories.

IV. Trauma Denied— The Survivor

WHAT MY MOTHER RECOUNTED: "I HAD TO KILL MYSELF."

On the homepage of the Suhrkamp Publishing House, the publisher of my mother's German-language books, a brief bio of my mother begins with the following lines: "Alice Miller was born on January 12, 1923, in Poland. In Basel, she studied philosophy, psychology and sociology. Upon obtaining her doctorate, she completed her training as a psychoanalyst and practiced this profession for 20 years. In 1980, she gave up her practice and teaching activity in order to write."

On my mother's homepage, one reads: "Alice Miller (January 12, 1923—April 14, 2010), PhD in philosophy, psychology, and sociology, as well as a researcher on childhood and the author of 13 books, translated into 30 languages, gave up her practice and teaching activity as a psychoanalyst in order to write."

When I read these words today, I am stunned, above all by what is omitted. The true drama of her life is nowhere to be found, the years of persecution are blanked out. Still, this is exactly what my mother abided by all her life. And not only that: she also allowed untruths to circulate about her life, even spread some of them herself. For instance, the matter of her supposed maiden name, Rostovska, as we know by now, was not her maiden name at all. Rostovska was her assumed name, the false identity that allowed her to survive in Warsaw from 1941 until 1945. She kept this name even after the war ended, and gave it to the immigration authorities in Switzerland. Why? She never explained.

That her family succeeded in smuggling her out of the Warsaw Ghetto and placing her under a false name with a Christian family, as can be read in Wikipedia, also does not correspond to the truth. It is also untrue that all her relatives could not escape murder in the Warsaw Ghetto. Why did Alice Miller never rectify these mistakes? I never asked her.

Only when I was about 41 years old did my mother tell me an incomplete outline from the time in the Warsaw underground. Her narrative contained a controlling aspect; in retrospect, it seems to me that she, while talking, was operating a system of censorship, in order to escape the situation and to not have to answer uncomfortable questions. She always remained silent about the years from 1939 until 1941, about what happened in her little hometown directly after the German assault on Poland.

As I remember it, her narrative vacillated in tone between great aggression—such as toward her mother and her sister, both of whom she assisted in the act of going underground and surviving—and great fear. In her account, her mother was again and again a mortal danger to them all, having been both passive and stubborn. Allegedly, she refused to deny her Jewish identity, which in 1941 made the search for a place to live very difficult, putting Alice in mortal danger as well. In any event, she blamed her mother for the fact that she fell into the hands of a blackmailer, who threatened to betray her to the German occupiers. She told me repeatedly, upset at the recollection, that she had to give the blackmailer her pearls, her "last jewelry," as payment. This, she insisted had been her mother's fault. Later, while writing the book, I often asked myself if this was the whole truth. Alice Rostovska was a very beautiful young woman, and I suspect that the blackmailer was not interested only in money and jewelry.

Anyway, as Alice Rostovska, she succeeded in organizing a hiding place for her mother in the country. She found shelter for her twelve-year-old sister in a convent near the Warsaw Ghetto. She even arranged for her sister to be baptized, in order to further safeguard her cover, and Alice recounted with indignation that her mother criticized her harshly for doing this, too. For a short time, Alice herself lived with the nuns, who knew, but guarded, her secret.

Though she was stingy with facts, my mother lavishly repeated to me, and stressed, her burden of total self-renunciation, her crucial survival strategy:

For fear of death I could no longer know at all who I was. I had to impose total self-control upon myself. Not only was I afraid of being recognized and killed by the Nazis as a Jewess, but I dreaded my own inner liveliness. I was simply afraid that I could not keep myself sufficiently under control. I felt like a mother who had to raise her child at any price not to embarrass his parents in public. I began to observe myself incessantly, above all I was most afraid of myself, no longer only of the external threats. I had to erase my whole biography. I had to tell myself time and again that I no longer may be a Jewess, but that I am a Polish woman. I had to change my name, I had to assume a Polish identity. I had to split off and forget anything that could have given me away. I had to transmute, I had to construct a new person out of myself, a false identity, in order to survive. I had to learn to show myself correctly in public as this new person. I sensed that even though I was alive, yet in some way I still had to kill myself in order to survive.

She told, and retold, another episode to me, to demonstrate the brutality of the enforced denial of her life:

Even though one lives in the underground, constantly exposed to frightening mortal danger, I still was also a young girl who did not want to neglect the need for some personal care. So I went outside and to a hairdresser to have my hair cut. Usually, this is an enjoyable activity that is really a banality of life. In the hair salon, I was suddenly scared to death. Behind me, a young woman exclaimed delightedly: "Hello, Alice, how are you? What are you doing in Warsaw?" I realized immediately that it was an old classmate from former times who recognized me. In this moment, I found myself in mortal danger and only complete self-renunciation remained for me as means of salvation. I responded as icily as I possibly could: "Excuse me, I think you are confusing me. I have no idea who you are. Certainly, this is a misunderstanding."

For me personally, those words were a terrible torment. This young woman was the only good and longtime friend of my childhood and youth. In this moment I knew that, for survival reasons,

I had finally obliterated my previous life and had become an artificial person, who in reality did not exist. In truth, I did not have a relationship with Alice Rostovska, my new Polish name. My name was Alicija Englard. But this life had ceased to exist.

What I Found Out: Alice Rostovska—Survival in Warsaw 1939–1945

On September 1, 1939, Poland was attacked by Hitler's army. First came the bombers. Piotrków was heavily bombarded. By September 4, 1939, the small town had been taken over by the Germans, the persecution of the Jews started immediately after.

Irenka Taurek, the daughter of Ala and Bunio, was then a little girl of five years. She remembers:

> We all were frightened to death by the airplane attacks. My parents, Ala and Bunio, your mother, her sister and their parents, the grandparents England and the parents of Bunio, we all fled into the nearby forest, where we sought protection against the bombs. After the first attacks, we went back home. Our house was still standing and we hoped that it all was just a bad dream. But two days later, the Germans started the all-decisive attack and once again we all fled into the forest. When we arrived there, there was a blazing fire because of the bomb attacks. I was standing with my parents on a

narrow forest path, the rest of the family was still hidden in the forest. Suddenly, a car showed up and a distant cousin of my father was sitting in it. His parents had a textile factory in Warsaw. This cousin already had a transit visa to Brazil in his pocket and asked my parents and me to join him in his car. At first, my parents refused the offer as they did not want to forsake the rest of the family. But the relative persuaded them to flee. They should think of the child, of me. We got into the car with a heavy heart. There was one more free place left in the car. Bunio, my father, wanted Alice to come with us. He believed that the war would last no longer than six months and that they would return soon. Then, Alice was sixteen years old and already quite grown up. She strongly objected and said that she could not let down her family. Many years later, Alice confessed to me how much she later regretted this decision. Her whole life, she thought, would have turned out differently had she gone along with us. So we drove in the direction of Lemberg, the first city in Ukraine, and left the rest of the family behind. They returned to Piotrków and for some of the family it meant their death sentence.

After the separation from Ala and Bunio, Alice and her family returned to the town. It is not possible to reconstruct in detail what happened to them after the occupation by the Germans. But the persecution of the Jews in Piotrków is described on the homepage *www.holocaustresearchproject.org*. With reference to this source, I will summarize the war history of the small town. From the published testimonies, one can imagine what my mother experienced in the Piotrków

Ghetto. Until the establishment of the ghetto on October 9, 1939, the family still lived in their familiar surroundings. Then Alice's family, like all the others, became dispossessed and had to move to another, much poorer part of town, the ghetto. At that time, six thousand Jews still lived in Piotrków. After a wave of arrests in the surrounding villages and towns, the population of the ghetto swelled to twenty-eight thousand people. By October 28, 1939, the district of the ghetto was surrounded by walls and heavily guarded. As in a prison camp, human beings were degraded and tortured and used for forced labor. Many died from starvation and sickness, or the consequences of forced labor. The poverty was indescribable. Sheer arbitrariness ruled, murders of the civilian Jewish population went unpunished. Bunio Zussman's parents were among the many who were murdered.

Hanka Ziegler, a nine-year-old girl, came with her family at the beginning of the war from Lodz to the ghetto of Piotrków. She had four siblings. Her personal narrative conveys an accurate impression of how appalling and threatening the living conditions in the ghetto were:

We all stayed in one little room, the seven of us. Another fourteen people came to the room at different times. I remember sleeping on a chair with one of my brothers, it was awful. My father got caught foraging for food and was put in prison—I never saw my father again. My brother Zigmund and I were the breadwinners—he was about fourteen.

We collected all the food—he and I started selling bread and potatoes—we didn't have anything else to sell. And then we started scavenging and begging from non-Jewish people. Being such small children we could get through any hole—we learned how to steal, how to beg. My mother was unable to do anything—she just couldn't cope. We were very hungry—so we went out of the ghetto—we went backwards and forwards—then the day came when they sealed the ghetto. (Holocaust Research Project.org)

Between June and July of 1941, the German occupation forces detected a Jewish underground organization inside the ghetto. The president of the Jewish council and its members were immediately arrested, tortured, and then deported to Auschwitz and murdered there. The people in the ghetto were told that the murder victims had all died of an illness.

But the underground organization continued working. There was even an underground paper which reported that Jews from Vilna and other places were abducted and deported to concentration camps. The death camps were in Chelmno and Treblinka. It was also reported that the occupying power intended to empty the ghettos, and that all the Jews were to be deported into camps and gassed there. No one wanted to believe this. It was too awful.

On October 13, 1942, all the remaining Jews in the vicinity of Piotrków were displaced to the ghetto. Then the Waffen-SS and the Ukrainian military under the leadership of SS-Hauptsturmführer Willy Blum closed in on the ghetto. At 2 PM on October 14, 1942, the "Operation" of the Waffen-SS began. Every house was searched and everyone was driven to the square in front of the great synagogue. Old and sick people were immediately shot. The others were rounded up on the main square and divided into two columns. Two thousand young men fit for work were provided with work passes and sent back to the ghetto. The remaining twenty-two thousand—old men, women and children—were packed into wagons and deported to Treblinka, where they were gassed.

Joshua Segal worked for three years as a forced laborer at the Hortensia factory. He recalls the selection of his family and the liquidation of the ghetto as follows:

> Everyone had to gather in the square. An SS-Officer ordered everybody to stand up, and all those who were working in some capacity were to stand to one side. My brother and I moved to where the officer indicated. An officer moved down the line and selected people to move to the left or right. Fathers and people who had work permits with Swastika approval went to the right, the rest of the families went to the left.

> When he came to my family, he separated my father from my mother and sisters, but my father refused to leave the family and said, "I go with my wife", and proceeded to go left. After the German officer had finished dividing the people, the soldiers surrounded the group and marched them away to the railway station and loaded them into cattle cars without food or water.

> They were told they were going to a labour camp. The train started down the tracks, going past the glass factory where I was working; I heard the train whistle, and knew without looking up what was in that train.

> But I did not know that my own family were in the boxcars, and that I would never see them again. I

was fifteen years old and my brother was nineteen
and we were alone. (Holocaust Research Project.org)

Abraham Dov Englard with his wife Sarah, my great-
grandparents, were also on this train to Treblinka. They
also perished in the gas chamber. Abraham is referred to
by name in a Spanish report about this transport, which I
found on the homepage of Yad Vashem.

This was Alicija Englard's world after September 1939. It
is inconceivable how great her fear, her despair must have
been. But nevertheless she succeeded to free her family, at
least her mother and sister, from the ghetto. Her cousin Ala,
the daughter of her aunt Franja, recounts:

> Alice was always so intelligent and bright. She always
> had a solution for everything. It was typical of her
> that she managed to save part of her family from
> the ghetto. Very soon she had a relationship with
> the underground organization. Through this orga-
> nization she connected with Poles outside of the
> ghetto. She could only consider surviving outside
> of the ghetto because she did not look very Jewish
> and spoke perfect Polish, which most Jews did not.
> So she obtained a passport with a false name: from
> then on her name was Alice Rostovska.

After she had escaped the ghetto (about July 1940) she
went to Warsaw where she registered in the underground
university. She taught as a student and earned money.
When her new life was established, she also obtained false
passports and identities for her mother Gutta and her sister Irena. She was thus able to free them from the ghetto

before the Great Selection of 1942. They had to leave father Meylech behind in the ghetto: he was gravely ill. Moreover, his Polish was too poor and would have given him away at once. He died there in 1941, alone, as a result of his illness.

What it meant to survive as a Jew in the "Aryan" part of Warsaw, the literary critic Marcel Reich-Ranicki has depicted in his book *The Author of Himself: The Life of Marcel Reich-Ranicki* (2002: Phoenix, an imprint of the Orion Publishing Group Ltd.). Only through his recollections have I been able to better grasp my mother's situation at the time; and I reference those recollections to better illustrate my mother's own situation: Reich-Ranicki was taken with his family and his future wife Tosia to the Warsaw Ghetto. He soon attained a position in the Jewish Council, which the Nazis had selected to organize the ghetto for the German occupational force, and act as a liaison with occupiers. There he worked as a translator, which gave him access to information vital for survival. He soon realized that the SS was determined to deport the residents of the Warsaw Ghetto to death camps and murder them there. Together with friends, they began to plan their escape from the ghetto:

> This endeavor was extraordinarily difficult and meant an enormous risk. Anyone outside the ghetto who knew of the existence of a Jew and did not immediately denounce him, who actually helped him and provided shelter for him, risked the death sentence, together with his family. The Jews discovered in the "Aryan" parts of the city—many had already fled before the "First Operation" (deportation to the ghetto) or had not gone to the ghetto in the first place—were usually shot on the spot. [Page 187] ...

The "Second Operation" to deport Jews from the ghetto to Treblinka was carried out on January 18, 1943. Reich-Ranicki and his wife, with a few friends, were able to escape from the line of people. They hid in the cellar of a house within the ghetto. Reich-Ranicki describes the potential for survival for a Jew in the "Aryan" part of Warsaw as requiring sheer superhuman effort:

> If, after the January deportations, one wished to escape certain death, one absolutely had to flee, and to flee as fast as possible, from the ghetto. But three prerequisites were necessary for a Jew to have any chance of survival in the "Aryan" part of town. First, one needed money or valuables to buy papers, not to mention the likelihood of being blackmailed. Second, one must not look Jewish and behave in a way that the Poles might suspect that one was Jewish. Third, one needed non-Jewish friends and acquaintances outside the ghetto, people prepared to help." [Page 190]

Disillusioned, Reich-Ranicki and his wife realized that they did not fulfill any of those survival conditions. With their friends, they managed nonetheless to procure money and then considered the flight more carefully. In doing so, Reich-Ranicki describes the odds of survival in the "Aryan" part of town as overwhelmingly slim:

> I did not seriously consider the possibility of fleeing to the "Aryan" part of the city.... I realized that every neighbor, every passerby, even a child, could denounce me. The probability of meeting my death outside the ghetto was, I believed, 99 per cent. Inside the ghetto, on the other hand, there was a 100 per

cent certainty of dying. I had to seize this minimal chance. [Page 191]

He describes further the life-threatening circumstances in the "Aryan" part of town:

> Thousands of Poles, often unemployed adolescents, who had grown up without completing their education, and many of whose fathers were in captivity, people who had not learned anything and had nothing to do, spent their days suspiciously watching all passersby: They were everywhere, especially near the ghetto boundary, looking for Jews, hunting down Jews. This pastime was their profession and probably also their passion. It was said that, even if there were no other signs, they were able to identify Jews by the sadness in their eyes. [Page 194]

So it was clear that only he, who managed to not be recognizable as a Jew, had a chance, albeit a very slim chance, of surviving. When he had to leave his hiding place, Reich-Ranicki choose the following "disguise":

> I obtained a *Völkischer Beobachter*, held it so that the front page with the swastika was clearly visible, and strode down the street briskly, with my head held high. The blackmailers and denouncers would, I hoped, take me for an eccentric German who had better not to be importuned. [Page 194]

This life-threatening game of hide-and-seek defined my mother's life as well between the ages of 18 and 22. Thanks to her contacts with the Polish underground, my mother knew that the underground army of Poles was planning an uprising against the Germans. When the Russians had already advanced to the banks of the Vistula, there was no holding the insurgents back any longer. The uprising began on August 1, 1944. It represented the largest single armed upheaval in occupied Europe during World War II. The resistance fighters fought 63 days against the German occupying forces before they had to capitulate in the face of a hopeless situation.

Twenty-one-year-old Alice and sixteen-year-old Irena used the turmoil of the uprising, their cousin told me, to cross the Vistula under huge fear of death, and reached safety in Russian-occupied territory. There, Alice worked in a military hospital until the end of the war. What she saw there reflected all the horrors of war.

After the war, Irena and Alice settled in Lodz. Their family was torn apart, and the many dead were mourned. Their grandparents had perished in the gas chambers at the Treblinka death camp. Dora, her aunt, died with her husband and son in the Warsaw Ghetto. Ala, Bunio, and little Irenka survived the flight through Russia, suffered deportation to Siberia, and forced labor, but they returned to Lodz in 1945. Franja and her family had found salvation for themselves in a trek through France, Spain, and Portugal, and eventually to America. Fisher, the eldest son, and his daughter Eva, fought alongside the Zionists in Palestine and championed the foundation of the state of Israel. Meylech, Alice's father, had died in the Piotrków Ghetto. Alice herself, her sister Irena and Gutta, the mother, had survived.

Surviving with the
False Self

Is it going too far to argue that my mother, in September of 1939, in the burning forest near Piotrków, elected to take responsibility for family, and in so doing gave up the freedom she had enjoyed as a child in the house of her relatives? Even though she never told me about this fateful moment in the forest, she never tired of lamenting that she had to be responsible for her parents' and sister's survival, even though she actually rejected her family. She felt that fate had forced her to demonstrate love for people she did not even like.

Since I have come to know the story of her decision, the background of her rage has become clear to me: Alice had much closer family bonds with Ala, Bunio, and Irenka than with her own family. These three had become her actual attachment figures. And now, in a life-threatening situation, she found herself faced with the choice of favoring her feelings or—as tradition demanded—sticking with her family. I think that when she decided for her family, she also took on the responsibility for their safety.

The decision of my mother to sacrifice herself for the family, although the decision ran at odds with her feelings for her family, can be seen as a typical instance of parentification of children by their parents. Alice, herself still a teenager, senses the helplessness of her parents and assumes the role of the adult. She cannot evade this task. I am convinced that this experience also guided my mother unconsciously when, decades later, she formulated in her books her theories and critique of parental behavior. That this moment was crucial is also substantiated by her confession with a feeling of deep shame to her cousin Irenka, not long before my mother's death, that she actually regretted the mission of rescuing her family during the war.

Nevertheless, the creation in the extreme of a false self during the war saved my mother's life. The tragic consequence of this traumatic experience was that Alice Miller permanently carried two different personalities within. On the one hand, the defiant, rebellious Alicija, who revolts against norms and who, already as a child, stands up for the existential right of human originality; and on the other hand, the almost invisible Alice, who absolutely obeys the coercion to adapt in order to ensure her survival. In addition, there was the tension of an essential paradox: the Jewish identity she had rejected now had to be hidden at any cost from her persecutors.

The later life of Alice Miller, as will be shown in subsequent chapters, was marked by the tension of moving continuously between these two extremes, exacerbated by the paradox of her Jewish identity. Again and again she found herself in totally other-directed life situations, in which she was forced to deny herself. Now and then she would find ways to free herself from a predicament, and tried to live as her own self. But she was always a prisoner of her deep-seated fear that she might be deprived of her freedom and forced back once again into the bondage of having to adapt to survive. When I once asked my mother in her old age why she had concealed her Jewish identity—and thus, mine as well—she responded:

> I was so terribly afraid that one day I could be arrested because I had hidden my Jewish identity under a false name. For decades, I was still afraid that the Nazis would come and imprison me in a concentration camp. It was plainly an unbearable idea for me having to reveal my true identity.

Alice Miller never overcame her war trauma; these horrible experiences, seared into her being, continuously shaped and defined her entire life.

Erwin Leiser (1923–1996), a journalist and filmmaker, relates in his book *Life After Survival* (1982: Königstein) and film of the same name, his encounters with, and the fates of, people who survived the Holocaust. He vividly points out how life goes on after survival. Primarily, it is a fight to stay alive at all. The survivors remain trapped in their experience and rarely manage to leave this prison. They remain lonely and feel completely misunderstood. They had been destined for death and can no longer find their way back into life.

His concise and compassionate words have helped me not only to recognize the hidden foundations of my mother's life after 1945, but also to reassess her behavior towards me. The principals that shape the lives of survivors function like laws set in stone. For me, they have answered the following questions:

1. Why was I confronted with this rejecting wall of silence? Why did I never dare to ask curious questions as a child?

The victims do not talk. The reasons for this silence are different. The victims know that no one who has not been in a camp himself can truly understand their experiences. *(Leiser, p. 12)*

2. Why could my mother never enjoy life? Why was it so difficult for her to tolerate company? Why did she become often aggressive for reasons inexplicable to me?

Elie Wiesel, who survived Auschwitz, attempts the following answer in Leiser's book:

They eat, they laugh, they love, they seek money, fame, recognition. Like the others. But it isn't true: they are playing, sometimes without even knowing it. ... These people have been amputated; they have not lost their legs or their eyes, but their joy of life. The things they have seen will come to the surface again, sooner or later. And then the world around them will be frightened and won't dare look these spiritual cripples in the eye. ... They are not normal people.

But they have to try to find their way among normal people.

Survivors want nothing more than to undo their experience. They erect a wall of silence and split off what they have experienced. They avoid any situation that reminds them of what they have been through. Unfortunately, they do not succeed, rather the next generation is woven into the split-off horror of those experiences and thus taken as hostages into captivity. This is my role in the persecution history of my mother: "The children of the victims of persecution learn that there are experiences in their parent's past which may not be talked about. ... Yet, by this silence, also the wounds are taken on by the next generation." *(Leiser, p. 13)*

V. Forced Love—The Wife

I never had a good relationship with my father. Andreas Miller, according to Wikipedia a Swiss sociologist and temporary husband of Alice Miller, was born Andrzej Miller on May 26, 1923, in Warsaw, and died on July 7, 1999, in Zurich. During the German occupation, he studied sociology, law, and economics at the Warsaw underground university. Otherwise, I don't know anything about his life during wartime German occupation of Poland. He obtained his doctorate in 1951 under Karl Jaspers and Edgar Salin; he received his university lecturing qualification in 1959. Then he taught as a private lecturer in Zurich, as a guest lecturer in Basel, and as of 1965, he was a professor of sociology at the University of St. Gallen. I was born in 1950. He was then twenty-seven years old—and, like my mother, a short time away from completing his doctoral degree. My parents lived in a very cramped space; a baby was a burden. One could also say we did not have a good start. I shall come back to this later.

I remember my father—he died in 1999 of a heart attack—as a man who was contemptuous, choleric, and authoritarian towards me. He brought me up, one could say, with carrots and sticks—like many children of that time. Which means I was often beaten, and on the other hand spoiled with my favorite meal. In any case, for me as a child, his moods were unpredictable. Why my father often had violent tantrums directed at me, I cannot answer. Today, I think that he had to act out the tensions in the relationship with my mother in this way. Due to his influence, I did not learn Polish and was raised a Roman Catholic.

Later—in the context of the divorce and thereafter—my father tried, though in vain, again and again, to make me his confidant. He badmouthed my mother at every opportunity, described himself as an unhappy lover and my mother as an ice-cold, calculating person. What I remember as particularly repulsive was his confession, long after the end of his marriage, that he was an anti-Semite. He expressed stereotypical prejudices about Jews, which I will not repeat here, but which were full of hatred for my mother.

My personal aversion for my father, it is clear to me, is the byproduct of several things: my mother's accounts of the early years of her marriage; the dirty war of divorce between my parents; and the toxic, condescending comments of my mother about her "blackmailer." The letter documented at the beginning of this book gives an idea of my mother's view of her husband.

I do not have a clear picture of how my parents' marriage looked from the inside, what bound them together during all those years, even though they were of so little good to each other. But like many children of broken marriages, I have experienced and sensed more of the destructive dynamics between my parents than was good for me. So I ask you to read the following depictions with my difficult position in mind.

Restrained Hatred—
The Marriage of
My Parents

My parents met in 1945, after the end of the war, at the University of Lodz, where my mother and her sister had begun their new lives. Alice was studying philosophy. It must have been a euphoric time in her life, looking forward, and driven by the absolute will to leave the horrors of war behind. She was twenty-two years old. She had survived the war. She plunged into life and learning.

Among her many admirers was also a fellow student, Andrzej Miller, a shy, uptight young man, full of complexes. Andrzej, as she would tell me later, admired Alice's beauty, but had to resign himself to the agonized feeling that with so much competition, he stood little chance of being noticed by this desirable woman. But he was tenacious and followed her at every turn. It was a disturbing coincidence that this admirer had the same name as the man who had black-mailed Alice during the war. One of the horrible anecdotes, which my mother told me casually long after her divorce, follows: "Your father had the same name as the man of the Polish Gestapo who had blackmailed and persecuted me during the war." And she added: "Only decades later, with the dreadful divorce, could I get away from your father, and thus also from my persecutor during the war."

Soon after 1945, the political climate in Poland deteriorated. After the Red Army had liberated Poland from German occupation, a Communist government was instituted in Poland under Wladislaw Gomulka. Frighteningly, a threatening anti-Semitism was soon rampant once more, unsettling the few Jews who had survived World War II. Bunio and Ala were planning to leave the country, and Alice wanted to get away, too. She applied, without success, for scholarships in the United States and France, but received one only from Switzerland. Emigration was decided upon, and she probably also hoped to get rid of her unloved admirer Andrzej. According to her cousin Irenka Taurek, to Alice he was little more than an intrusive fellow student. For my father, however, the situation looked quite different. When he was already at war with my mother—a full-blown divorce war—he told me: "I loved your mother above all else, but she was cold as ice and showed no consideration for me. Without my knowledge, she applied for scholarships abroad and received one for Switzerland. She let me know only one week before her departure. I was beside myself because I did not want to lose her." He then applied for a scholarship himself, but it was not possible at such short notice. Finally, Andreas persuaded a fellow student to concede to him his own scholarship for Switzerland. "And so it happened that your mother and I flew to Switzerland, to Basel." It was a triumph for him.

My mother, in turn, later confided to me her shock at discovering that Andrzej was following her to Switzerland. Her cousin Irenka, however, recalled the relationship still in markedly different terms: "Since the departure from

Poland, they both showed themselves as a couple in love. They strolled around holding hands. One could not help thinking that they truly loved each other."

And yet, irritating questions remain: Did my mother already then feel persecuted, did the experience trigger the old fears, was she forced to put up a brave front to appease the new "persecutor?" Outwardly, everything seemed perfect, but if I trust my mother's account, her inner emotional state was the exact opposite.

As a therapist, I have been frequently confronted with this phenomenon in couples counseling: the couple that appears harmonious on the outside, while destructive emotions rage under the surface. Such couples had no spark at all at the beginning of the relationship. Often, the woman initially has had no interest in a relationship, but ultimately succumbed to the man's persistent courtship. By some circumstance, she finds herself in a dependent position and accepts with gratitude that she is no longer alone. But beneath the surface of gratitude, feelings of resentment begin to grow.

In the case of my parents, I think Alice was pleased, despite her reluctance toward her suitor, to have someone from her homeland by her side during a stressful time of emigration. Andrzej stood by her at just the right moment, upon leaving Poland. She was homesick, felt uprooted and lonely, and longed for comfort and security. He was the connection with the homeland, he became the placeholder for all that she had missed during the last years, during the war. And he took advantage of the dependency and could finally be with my mother; he became—at least in his perception—her protector in a foreign land.

But his happiness—and I am sure that he was happy about his conquest—hardly endured. The marriage of my parents, at least from my own perspective, was marked by aggression. I can count on one hand the times when I observed my parents interacting normally and in an easy manner. Otherwise, arguments prevailed in the Miller household or, at the very least, an uncomfortable tension.

My mother later gave me the impression that Andrzej, who soon called himself Andreas in Switzerland, had had frantic fears of loss. He had pursued her jealously, regularly making scenes in front of her. Over and over again, she had wanted to separate, but failed. Tearfully, he had begged her to stay. He had argued, again and again, that one should not separate in a foreign land, that after all that had happened during the war, one should not revoke solidarity. And time and again, she had returned to him.

In 1949, after both had finished their courses of study, they married. If I believe my mother, she married reluctantly, but also from a feeling of distress. She longed for calm, for normality, and probably also hoped that the constant dramas of jealousy would come to an end. But the destructive dynamic remained a problem. After their studies, they both decided to pursue their doctorates. They lived in a tiny flat at Lake Zurich, and each one worked on their doctorate. Added to the emotional tensions were the cramped conditions. Both of them had to study, write, and live in one room. There was no heat, winter was cold. It is not hard to imagine what the tensions were like between them as they had to write their dissertations with those negative feelings in such a confined space. Furthermore, they competed with each other. Andreas was more systematic, but intellectually rather less flexible than his wife. Alice was already then gifted with the ability to recognize connections in a creative way, and with lightning speed. She had a playful approach, completely unlike Andreas. Presumably, he felt intellectually inferior to his wife. Despite, or precisely because of it, he apparently tried to force her, over and over, to take on his systematic approach. In a struggle familiar from her childhood, she defended her right to live according to her own precepts and ideas. The relationship degenerated into an unceasing fight for self-determination. Andreas became obsessed with paranoid fears of loss, while his wife felt her inner freedom threatened by his restrictions and regulations. It seems that mutual hatred shaped the relationship more and more. It is barely comprehensible how, in such a poisoned climate, they could have a mutual desire to conceive a child. Yet, in April of 1950, I was born. Probably they both felt a deep desire for peace and fell victim to the illusion that founding a family would reduce or even resolve their relationship problems.

As they both were burdened by their war trauma, they may have also wanted to reassure themselves that they had truly survived. It is a mark of survivor defiance, so to speak, to shake off murderous persecution by having a child. My sister Julika came into the world in 1956. She was a child with Down's Syndrome, which had already occurred in my father's family, a fact he had kept a secret my mother. She never forgave him. Then, the family literally exploded. Julika spent her first year in a home, and I was also put into a children's home for two years.

I always experienced my parents as extremely tense and constantly preoccupied with themselves. My father worked day and night, my mother tried desperately to seize a sphere of freedom for herself, in order to escape the jealous grasp of her husband. Upon entering the world of psychoanalysis in 1953, her true liberation from him began. She began to claim a territory of her own. Still, this did not put an end to the destructive and callous arguments of my parents, which were virtually the background noise of my childhood. The situation worsened during the years after 1960, when my parents hosted the open house of an ascending academic family. In her accounts to me, my mother presented herself as the driving force in all these social contexts. My father, she said, was of little use in such matters; she compared his mental capabilities with those of her mother.

I was too young to be in a position to judge this. I remember the guests, of course, and the lively conversations. My parents socialized with scholars of the university, discussing poems by Hölderlin, or philosophers and their themes. They succeeded in forming something like a salon. In doing so, my mother made sure that her friends from the psychoanalytic seminar also visited regularly. In this manner, she weaved a network of relationships that enabled her to distance herself more and more from my father. To the outside world, the marriage functioned; they were friendly hosts, and appeared to be an intellectual couple. But the more the conflicts at home escalated, the more my mother fled into the world of psychoanalysis. She alone had true access to this world, while my father and we children remained bystanders. The facade was perfect, and they maintained it for almost twenty years more. Only after a severe bout with breast cancer did my mother find the strength to demand a separation and see it through. Their divorce in the year 1973, after twenty-four years of marriage, came far too late.

LOVE AND THE STOCKHOLM SYNDROME

The erratic relationship of my parents, at least the behavior of my mother, can perhaps best be understood in the context of Stockholm syndrome. This term refers to the adjustment of hostages to their captors. The phenomenon described by this term goes back to a hostage-taking in Stockholm in 1973, during which the hostages built a positive emotional relationship with their captors. The term fell into established German-language use in 1975, after the occupation of the German embassy in Stockholm by German terrorists. There, one of the female hostages fell in love with the terrorist captor.

In a state of helplessness and powerlessness, a hostage clings desperately to this survival strategy. By unconditional devotion to the captor, the hostage can to an extent save herself, experiences the threat as less existential. The hostage no longer feels completely at the mercy of the captor. It also happens that a hostage identifies with the terrorist actions; indeed, even becomes a terrorist himself or herself, to ward off the feeling of absolute dependency. The hostage is no longer completely passive, but regains the ability of action.

It seems obvious to me that Alice Miller experienced the possessive love of Andreas Miller in a manner similar to

71

someone who has been taken hostage. She herself identified him with her blackmailer during the war years; one indication is her prolonged inability to separate earlier from him. Later, she would often tell me that she had, from the very beginning, felt like a prisoner, and like someone under constant surveillance. Andreas managed indeed to bind her to himself over and over. For one thing, he stoked her fears that she would not be able to survive in a hostile, unfamiliar environment without him. For another, he seduced her by repeatedly providing feelings, however transient, of security. The alleged love of Andreas Miller seems to me like control driven by fear of loss. It is evident to me that my mother, on an emotional level, latched unconsciously to feelings that she knew from her time of suffering in the "Aryan" part of Warsaw. The feeling of dependence, which she had experienced with her "blackmailer" in order to survive, repeated itself. By now, I understand the "hostage-taking" by her husband as a continuation of her war trauma.

VI. Alienated by Choice—
The Woman Emigrant

A New Life in Switzerland
1946–1985

The university scholarship in Switzerland, as previously noted, was not my mother's first choice. It was her emergency exit out of a Poland that remained dangerous for Jews even after the war had ended and the German occupying forces were gone. My mother would have much rather emigrated to France or the United States, but the institution that awarded scholarships decided differently. Ala, Bunio, and Irenka, who had survived the war in a Siberian prison camp, accompanied my mother. And—as I have already pointed out—so did the man who later became my father.

Irenka describes the departure from Poland as follows:

From Lodz, we drove to Warsaw. The city was still in ruins from the war. We knew that we would fly to Zurich with a Swissair flight. We had the opportunity to spend the night in the noble Hotel Bristol in Warsaw. It was the only hotel which the Germans had not destroyed because they had used it themselves. I will never forget how well we were accommodated there, and how well we ate. Then we departed on time from Warsaw and left Poland, despite everything our beloved homeland, for a long time. We landed in Zurich, and my parents were welcomed by a cousin of my father. Alice and Andreas immediately drove on to Basel, while my parents moved to Locarno and spent their initial time in Switzerland in Ticino.

Mother Gutta and sister Irena, meanwhile, moved to Warsaw in 1946, where Irena lived with her future husband, Richard. They have a son, Marek, who lives in Warsaw today. Irena studied ethnology and did research in this field. Richard made a career in the Communist Party and became ambassador to different countries; during the 1960s, he lived with his family in Mexico. Initially, Irena stayed in Mexico and taught at the university, while her husband and son returned ahead of her to Poland. Gutta lived out the rest of her life with Irena's family; Irena, who divorced Richard after her return from Mexico, cared for her mother until her death.

To arrive from war-ravaged Poland to undamaged Switzerland was a culture shock. Andreas and Alice could hardly grasp that they had landed in a country where the war had not taken place. My mother often spoke of one incident that occurred shortly after their arrival, because it seemed monstrous beneath its veneer of smug banality:

> We were invited for dinner to a restaurant. Very intimidated and deeply impressed we sat down at the table. It was basically unimaginable for me that after the war, after the deprivations which I had experienced, there could be a place anywhere in this world where people could matter-of-factly sit at a table and eat to their heart's content. I noticed particularly

a family at the neighboring table: they had a huge bowl with a steaming soup in front of them— but the father was narcissistically reading a newspaper. He had a cigar in his mouth and a big pot belly. His wife sat timidly next to him and did not disturb him while he was reading, also the children did not say a word. They seemed to me like little lapdogs that did not dare to move. Finally the father served himself soup and ate with such self-evident satisfaction that it seemed abysmally arrogant to us. We thought we had landed on the moon. I was so shocked at what I saw there.

Later, she interpreted this first encounter as a key experience for her permanent feeling of alienation towards Switzerland and the Swiss. "I was never happy in this country," she stated more than once to me. Even though she tried for decades to adapt, she remained—so it seemed to her—a stranger.

Alice and Andreas each found accommodation with host families in Basel and began their course of study in philosophy at the local university. The host families in Basel belonged, according to my mother, to the highest social class. Their wealth seemed downright obscene to her after the deprivations of war. She could get very agitated when she spoke about this. At that time, I did not yet know anything about the prosperity of her family of origin. Today, I ask myself if her indignation contained the resonance of grief over what she had lost during the war. Besides, the "refugees" were probably kept in rather barren conditions by their "benefactors." My mother recalled her lodging in Basel as an especially humiliating experience. Overall, the refugees were clearly made to feel that, although they were tolerated, they were by no means loved. In addition, nobody was really interested in what they had experienced during the war. With astonishment and extreme discomfort, my mother found that the Swiss with whom she had contact were often oblivious to what had happened in World War II.

My mother studied philosophy with great interest, and even then began to take a strong interest in psychology. Many intellectuals and artists, who wanted to escape persecution by the Nazis, had saved themselves by fleeing to Switzerland, which had remained neutral during the war. There were many top talents, also at Basel University. The theological and philosophical faculties comprised many particularly famous scholars, among them theologian Karl Barth and existentialist philosopher Karl Jaspers. Alice thrived in this world and enjoyed hours of exuberant freedom. At the same time, she often felt lonely. Books became her refuge. When she was unhappy, she withdrew with her books and shut herself off from the rest of the world. This is what she had already done as a child. With the help of books she could create a world of her own, where she could do as she wanted, and where no one could bother her.

Andreas Miller was the director of the Polish Museum in Rapperswil at Lake Zurich, from 1948 until the museum closed in 1952. This establishment, which had operated since 1875, with intermittent periods of closure, had been an important place for many Polish emigrants, a conservator of Polish national identity during that country's annexation. Since 1936, it had functioned as a museum for contemporary Poland, and had organized cultural events during the war for the thirteen thousand Polish soldiers interned in Switzerland. The period of Andreas's directorship of the museum comprised my parents' wedding (1949), my birth

(1950), my mother's graduation, and her work on her doctoral thesis, supervised by Heinrich Rickert, on the subject of "The Problem of Individual Concept Formation," which was finally published in 1955.

During the years in Rapperswil, my parents gave the outward appearance of successful integration, although my mother always disputed this. In her memory, the feeling of alienation remained dominant. On the outside, she acted as hostess, inwardly she felt out of place and like a stranger. As a matter of fact, my parents were part of an intellectual, bourgeois circle of friends, which included, it was said, the academic and economic grandees of Rapperswil. And while Alice and Andreas were part of this circle, they were by no means able to keep up financially with the others in their social group. Maybe it was impossible for my mother to become rooted because of an unconscious yearning for the part of her life that the Nazis had ripped from her? My parents' life in Switzerland reminds me of the lifestyle cultivated by Ala and Bunio Zussman in the academic world of Piotrków, where Alice always had felt very comfortable. Could it be that the persistent feeling of alienation was also due to the reality that the new friends could never be more than a stale substitute for the lost world, a symbolic memory of a time that was irrevocably lost? It is a question that remains unanswerable.

In the scheme of things, my mother ended up living nearly forty years in Switzerland. It is clear that she made both friends and enemies during this time, and that she put down roots, if not in the soil of Switzerland, then at least in the intellectual world which became accessible to her in Zurich in the Psychoanalytical Association (Chapter VII). My mother nevertheless disputed this point of view.

Provence, Place of Longing
1985–2010

In 1985, Alice Miller left Switzerland and moved to Saint-Rémy-de-Provence in southern France. While attending a congress in Aix-en-Provence in previous years, she had fallen in love with this region and began to dream of living there. At first, from 1985 until 1987, she rented a little house; in 1987, she then bought a house on a spacious property, situated outside of the village in a tranquil place, near the overgrown Jewish cemetery. Finally, she had found her place in the world, the place of her heart's desires. She was surrounded by a big olive grove, created a beautiful garden and had a small swimming pool installed. She redesigned the house according to her ideas. Finally she had found her nest, after long years of fleeing, of persecution, and feeling estranged. She enjoyed the view of the mountains of Provence and felt a kinship with the great impressionists, who painted their beautiful paintings in this special light. She could dedicate herself to painting and writing, and finally had found peace. She took long walks during which she could calmly be with her thoughts and plan new projects.

Alice lived in southern France for twenty-five years. She maintained contact with the world via books, letters, newspaper articles and later via the internet. She preferred written communication. Saint-Rémy-de-Provence became a haven. But after only a few years, her self-constructed nest turned into a hiding place, where she had to conceal herself from persecutors whom she still feared.

Virtual Messages from the Hiding Place—The Internet

The new digital media were a blessing for Alice Miller. My mother soon recognized and used the great potential of the internet for herself. During the last five or six years of her life, she used primarily the internet to socialize with her readers and other interested parties. This suited her purposes in a number of ways, not the least enabling her to keep to herself and forestall direct contact with other people. She remained hidden, invisible, but she was still connected to the outside social world through her website. Furthermore, she had a media platform to communicate her thoughts instantly, unfiltered and uncensored. She was very flexible, could react at once to criticism and comment on current issues. Yet she still kept control over the communication process.

It amazes me how quickly my mother in her advanced age understood the mechanisms of the internet, and how deftly she took advantage of the new medium. Instinctively, she also recognized the dangers of this medium and managed to avoid any major mistakes. During these years, my mother and I had scarcely any contact. But I often visited her website. I was very interested in how she maintained contact with her readers and how she tried to spread her ideas.

Above all, my mother used her website for therapeutic advice. Many people in need wrote to Alice Miller and shared the stories. My mother chose exemplary letters, published them on the internet, responded with advisory comments where she promoted her theories. Her readers were given the opportunity to become more familiar with Alice Miller's ideas by means of concrete examples. In point of fact, this also served to skillfully promote her books.

When I read my mother's comments, however, I was often left unpersuaded. They contradicted my practical experience as a therapist. I often wondered what positive synergies could have been occurred had my mother been able to work in partnership with me. But our relationship was too burdened for this. My mother preferred to analyze artists, poets, and philosophers post mortem, rather than test her theories on real people in direct conversation. She conducted her post-mortem analyses with great persuasiveness. Naturally, any analysis involving fictional psychotherapeutic treatment is theoretical and speculative, and the success of treatment can never be verified independently. Yet, thanks to the brilliant literary abilities of my mother, this drawback escaped notice. She knew very well how to sell her mental experiments as reality.

Similarly, her advice by letter on her website was conducted according to this scheme. The contents of the readers' letters were mostly reports on how they were mistreated as children by their parents, emotionally traumatized, sexually abused, or victims of brutal violence. They would tell how afraid they were to deal with their parents, and it often became apparent that they protected the parents, or simply were unable to confront their parents with their deeds. Often when I read my mother's responses to these letters, I felt discomfort. In all her answers, Alice Miller took a very

clear position: she asked the letter-writers to defend themselves against the parents and to confront them concretely
with their actions. I felt betrayed when I read these responses
because when I confronted my mother, she not only totally
rejected my criticism but, as I shall describe later, severed
her relationship with me.

The more my mother used the internet, the more isolated
and lonely she became in her self-chosen exile in Provence.
She began to perceive the world increasingly through the
distorted lens of the internet. Her public confrontations
became increasingly fundamentalist. She rejected any form
of criticism and reacted in an authoritarian manner. Her
behavior ultimately confused her readership, which became
increasingly polarized, with ardent admiration on one side,
and categorical rejection on the other.

   During the last six years of her life, she withdrew almost
completely from the world. She finally gave up her permanent residence in Switzerland, which she had kept until
2005, and settled decisively in France.

About the Impossibility of a New Beginning

Emigration marked a deep turning point in the life of my mother. It is the clearest expression of the decisive will for a new beginning, a repression of the past which has become geographical. My mother's most stringent daily routine calls for tremendous repression. But she does not quite succeed in escaping her trauma in this way. Again and again, it takes hold of her. Her mood changes, the feeling of being uprooted, clinging to the unloved husband—all this speaks to the impossibility of simply forgetting what has happened. Today, there is a term for these symptoms: PTSD, post-traumatic stress disorder. This was compounded—seemingly paradoxically—by the shock that nobody in her new world wanted to know what she had truly experienced. Many people shared this fate after World War II. Regardless of nation or religion, all were confronted by the same phenomenon. Whether perpetrator or victim, they had to keep what they had been through, their bad experiences, to themselves. No matter where they turned, no one was interested in their experience. How many people after 1945 were left on their own and had to heavily bear their fate? How many people never received affection and understanding, much less comfort, when it came to their war experiences?

Thus they became victims of the war for the second time. They had to try to block out everything in order to begin a whole new life.

However, this type of repression only works if one establishes a whole new personality. It is this dissociative behavior of the war generation which runs like a common thread through their biographies. Alice Miller is a typical example of this attempt to overcome traumatic war experiences. It is no wonder that in this process Switzerland could never become a real home for her. Only her subsequent life in southern France gave her a brief, and self-deceptive, feeling of security. She carried the war within herself, the wounds of trauma, and even in exile in Provence, true peace eluded her to the end of her life.

VII. FOUND FREEDOM—THE CHILDHOOD RESEARCHER

The period when my mother wrote her three most important books was the happiest time of my life in regard to our relationship. The memory nourishes me to this day; indeed, I would even go so far as to say that I found my calling as a psychotherapist during those good years with her. I was in my late twenties and early thirties and had been working for eight years as an elementary school teacher; I was standing on my own two feet, I was neither child nor competitor. My Mother found in me an empathic listener, into whose ears she could organize her thoughts, and to whose eager countenance she could develop her theories. Maybe it was also her way of saying "I am sorry." Because the topic of her books, the destructive power of parents over their children, described indeed a part of my lost childhood.

When my mother, fifty-six-years-old in 1979, turned to writing, a new period of her life began. She had freed herself from her unhappy marriage and gained a new foothold. She was about to challenge the orthodoxy of psychoanalysis with a concept of her own devising. The woman I recall from this time was happy and fully in touch with herself, imbued with a new-found ability to write; and she took me, her son, along in this fascinating process. For several years, we actually had peace.

MY MOTHER AS A
PSYCHOANALYST 1953–1978

Alice Miller began her training as a psychoanalyst in 1953, when I was three years old. At that time, there was no set institutional framework for this career path. But she soon got in touch with a renowned group of analysts who had gathered around Gustav Bally (1893–1966), psychiatrist and professor of psychotherapy. From this group would emerge, in 1958, the Psychoanalytic Seminar Zurich. Among those who accompanied Bally were also the two founders of ethnopsychoanalysis: psychoanalysts and ethnologists Paul Parin (1916–2009) and Fritz Morgenthaler (1919–1984). The entry into this intellectually astute and inspired milieu must have been a salvation for my mother. There she could breathe freely, I think, for the first time after many years. This peer group became her intellectual and emotional center until the mid-1970s. Thanks to this footing, I assume, was she able to bear her private difficulties at all. It strikes me as a mirror of her childhood experience, when she found refuge from the quarrels with her parents in the liberal home of her uncle and aunt. As she had done as a child, Alice Miller found once again a means of escape from a stressful family situation.

One must bear in mind that, at the time, the beginning of the 1950s, psychoanalysis had a different allure than it has today. Its practitioners were seen as avant-garde, its views an assault on bourgeois propriety, and it was a magnet for artists and intellectuals. When people underwent psychoanalysis at that time, it was more commonly to learn more about oneself as a person than to change neurotic behavior. Psychoanalysis was still regarded more as an exciting theory than a form of clinical therapy. The psychological theory, which was used to explore the dynamic of the psyche and its inner world, was compelling and mind-expanding.

My mother put a lot of time into her training, and very soon began her own psychoanalytical practice. Until 1964, she had a small practice high up in Zurich Niederdorf, in the old town. As a youth I visited her there several times. It was a pleasant place. Today I would say that one could sense how comfortable and liberated she felt there. Her office made me think of a small eagle's nest: a little room with a psychoanalyst's couch and a comfortable armchair. There were no pictures and no plants; there was simply not enough room. But at least she was enthroned high above the roofs of Zurich's old town. Here, Alice Miller began her private practice as a psychoanalyst. In tandem with her practical work, she remained in close contact with the psychoanalytical community, was a frequent guest in the "Kränzli" (a small circle of psychoanalysts who met regularly for discussions), and attended courses at the Psychoanalytical Seminar, which commenced in 1958. There, experienced psychoanalysts gave lectures and trained prospective practitioners.

The training included undergoing analysis, which was retroactively accredited as a training analysis after the final examinations—something uniquely Swiss. My mother found a female psychoanalyst who attended to her. She described to me this first analysis as a "complete catastrophe." She had expected great things from it, including help in dealing with her possessive husband, all the more so as she probably was having an affair at the time. But my mother felt that the analyst evinced no sympathy for her burdened emotional state. The analyst instead stressed how much my father was suffering, and how much of a burden he had assumed on behalf of the family. Ultimately, she advised my mother to reconcile with her husband. And eventually, my mother followed the advice, not least because she did not dare to contradict the analyst, as her professional standing depended on a successful analysis. She had denied herself in order to save a piece of freedom and independence, or so she deemed later.

Alice Miller ended this training analysis in 1955. She completed a second course of analysis with Gertrud Boller-Schwing, and then entered into longtime supervision work. Alice treated patients, and worked part-time several hours a week as an analyst in Zurich. At the beginning of the 1960s, she was accepted into the Swiss Society for Psychoanalysis.

During the early 1960s, psychoanalytical theory experienced the first of several great shocks. Orthodox psychoanalysis was put under enormous pressure by creative researchers within the profession's own ranks, and the faithful disciples of Freud began to push back. During this time, my mother worked as a psychoanalyst, and was also active as a training analyst and instructor at the seminar. She had become a well-established figure within the Swiss Society of Psychoanalysis; she had made it. The feeling of belonging was no doubt important to her. But it was not in her nature to accept uncritically everything placed in front of her. On the contrary: the more she felt sure of the world of psychoanalysis as her home, the more courageous and creative she became. Similar to the child who had scrutinized the orthodox rules of her parents, she now began to study the critics of psychoanalysis and pose critical questions herself. She was intrigued by the attempts of Austrian-American Heinz Kohut to integrate his findings into psychoanalysis, which caused downright trench warfare and ended in his expulsion from Freudian organizations. The orthodox know-it-all attitude of some colleagues must have been highly suspect to my mother; those colleagues must have struck her as akin to religious zealots who attacked frontally anyone who criticized their "faith." It was terrible for her that colleagues resisted changing and developing psychoanalysis in light of new findings, that new discoveries were systematically rejected and countered with outrageous arguments. But every opinion critical of orthodox psychoanalysis was treated as apostasy by the expanded "Kränzli" group, which Alice regarded as her family. She had to endure seeing Sigmund Freud, father of psychoanalysis, revered like a saint, whose theories were treated by the members of the psychoanalytic organizations as laws to be slavishly obeyed. What a strange, what a painful feeling of déjà vu for my mother. Psychoanalysis was no longer a refuge for the freedom of thought, but the bulwark of an ideological, intolerant, religiously worshipping mentality. Compliance with the rules was more important for the majority of Freudians than the innovative development of theory. Psychoanalysis and its organizations solidified into a closed system.

How did my mother react? She emigrated—inwardly, for the time being. By then, she had already developed a different style as an analyst, as Alexander Moser, a psychoanalyst who worked for years together with my mother in supervision, told me:

Your mother surprised me again and again during
case reviews because she developed with phenom-
enal empathy, after short examples of depictions of
transference or counter-transference, precise concepts about corresponding childhood situations of
the analysands, which could subsequently be con-
firmed by more association material and thus were
of big help for the analytic work of reconstruction
and construction. Precisely in this respect I have
learned a lot from your mother.

My mother's estrangement from classical psychoanalysis was
progressing, even if only in secret. She read authors who were
shunned by the psychoanalytical community for ideological
reasons, and in them she found answers to the questions that
concerned her own life. Three men in particular—Heinz
Kohut, John Bowlby, and Donald Winnicott—paved the way
for her own thinking. All three were interested in one theme:
how does a personality develop from the cradle on, and what
kind of relational experience does a human require from the
outset in order to acquire a self, a perception of oneself?

The English pediatrician and analyst Donald
W. Winnicott (1896–1971) considered external influences as
dangerous for the early development of a child in cases when
coercion to adjust to the needs of the environment stifles
the development of the self, of one's originality. Winnicott
understands the true self as the constitutional potential of
a human striving for development. Human beings develop
a false self in order to protect their inherent potential. In
order to protect their originality, human beings, if need be,
accept a life-long estrangement from themselves.

John Bowlby (1907–1990), the British pediatrician, child
psychiatrist, and pioneer of attachment research, studied

the mother-child relationship and found that a healthy self-development depends primarily on the intact relationship experience of the child with the mother. He opposed psychoanalysis because he ascertained from his research that the early mother-child relationship is more relevant for psychic development than what Freud had described as the sexual drive development. Bowlby was clearly of the opinion that environmental influences have a greater impact on the psychic development of a human being than the intrapsychic mastery of psychosexual conflicts.

The Austrian-American analyst Heinz Kohut (1913–1981) realized during his work as an analyst that children are, at a very early age, existentially dependent on being perceived by their social environment. He was one of the first psychologists who recognized how important social mirroring is for human psychic development. By no means did he consider the narcissistic needs of the infant, indeed of humans in general, as neurotic. Instead, he saw these needs as very important: every human being has an existential need to be appreciated through being mirrored as a person.

It is obvious why my mother was so attracted to these very authors in psychology. They focused on themes which had played a great role in her life—I cannot judge if she was conscious of this while reading their works. Probably not, because she herself later claimed that she only later became conscious of the role her mother had played in her childhood. But looking back from an outside perspective, the connection is immediately revealed: the experiences with the cold, emotionally limited mother caused a narcissistic insult to little Alice that had consequences. All her life, my mother remained incapable of dealing with criticism, and relived in every criticism the childhood rejection.

She took every criticism of her opinion personally, felt most profoundly rejected, and shot back mercilessly.

Her own experience of having to deny the true self must have seemed terribly familiar to her in the insights of Winnicott—both as a child in her family, and even more so intensified during the years of wartime persecution, when she was forced for survival reasons to reinvent herself as another person entirely.

Bowlby's work made her painfully aware of how much she had missed the secure attachment to her mother.

I can imagine very well that in reading these psychological authors, my mother's longing for her lost childhood intensified strongly, as did the rage directed at those who had denied her a childhood. Must these books not have sounded like testimonies of an unreal vision? What would it have been like to have had a happy childhood? Behind the attraction the thinking of these three colleagues had for her, must there not have been a great pain that either stayed hidden, or became revealed to her? At any rate, she found in their writings the themes around which my mother's later life's work revolved: self-worth (Kohut); the right of the child to develop his original self in the protection of a loving parental relationship (Winnicott); and the enormous importance of the emotional attachment to the primary caregiver (Bowlby).

All three authors had, in their theoretical writings, departed from classical psychoanalysis. It would go beyond the scope of this book to relate how the psychoanalytical community received their work. It should be noted, however, that through their research they revolutionized developmental psychology. They postulated that psychic disturbances are not the consequence of intra-psychic, unresolved sexual conflicts, but can be traced back to stressful, negative experiences in the relationship with the primary caregiver. From their work, it can be concluded that psychic disturbances are based on traumatic childhood experiences which, coming from the outside, fundamentally damage a healthy psychic development.

These theorists changed the very role of the analyst. Kohut, for instance, brought the concept of empathy into play. No longer was Freud's theory the final word in the analyst's relationship with patients; instead empathic access to patients became valued. This changed the content of analysis: the emotional state was to become the central focus of the sessions, no longer repressed conflicting drives. The relationship with the patient should be close and emotional, no longer detached and clinical. Mirroring the emotional experience of the patient was regarded as the most important therapeutic tool. The orthodox Freudians refused Kohut's approach point-blank and accused him of virtual heresy. The disputes took on the ideological features of a religious war; nevertheless, a new branch developed within psychoanalysis, self-psychology.

For my mother, the narrow-minded rigidity and fundamentalist ideology of the psychoanalysts who took issue with Kohut came as a shock. It is curious how she dealt with the problem of discovering that her new family of choice, at least its leading representatives, turned out to be fundamentalist. One could say she opened a secondary battlefield.

While the dispute over Kohut and other psychological researchers was raging, there was agitation by left-wingers, inspired by the so-called "68-ers" (the German student protest movement that began in 1968), to assume management of the Psychoanalytic Seminar Zurich. Of the founders of the institute, Parin and Morgenthaler sided with the left and imposed self-administration practically from the top down. My mother began, probably at first the only one in the seminar, to oppose this ideological onslaught from the left. She attacked the Marxist wing of the psychoanalysts, who wanted to change the conservative, hierarchical training policy. She defended vehemently the conservative elders, although she herself had begun to bid farewell to classical psychoanalysis with regard to content—because the conservative trends were too narrow-minded for her as well.

Alexander Moser, who then belonged to the inner circle of the Swiss Society for Psychoanalysis, described to me the situation at the time like this:

> Because of her special life-experience, your mother was sensitized to the epidemic dissemination of dominant political ideologies and therefore reacted with rare clarity and determination to the anarchist Marxist tendencies, which prevailed among the Freudian analysts in Zurich during the seventies—especially when well-known analysts could not separate from the little red book of Mao Tse-tung or raved about Fidel Castro, and treated everyone, who did not share their opinion, as a reactionary, petty bourgeois idiot, who had not understood the course of world history and thus represented an annoying obstacle to the progress of humanity. She also saw through the undemocratic claims to power behind political theories that were presented in a seemingly clever and complicated way, and how these were incompatible with a psychoanalytical educational institution. She was the first one to open the eyes of the members in the Swiss Society of Psychoanalysis

for the untenable development of the psychoanalytical training situation in Zurich, which finally led to a split of the seminar in 1977.

For me, my mother's effort has a familiar luster: Alice Miller once again demonstrates her talent for saving her "family"—as unloved as the family may be—from a totalitarian, this time Marxist threat. History repeats itself: the line-toeing, authoritarian, religiously blinded psychoanalysts are defended against the Marxist ideological attack.

At that time, I witnessed this dispute only as an observer from a distance, but I remember well the aggressive emphasis with which my mother fought her battle. Today I assess this defensive battle of my mother against the Marxists, and the "rescue" of the Psychoanalytical Society from a leftist takeover, in another light. If one accepts that in terms of her thinking, she had already embarked on a course that would alienate her from her colleagues in the psychoanalytical community, one must conclude that she had not yet found the resolve herself to break with her "family."

THE PATH TO FREEDOM

B etween 1973 and 1978, the tension between her inner convictions and the compulsion to adapt to the rigid rules of psychoanalysis must have become an ever greater emotional burden for my mother. In addition, there were the constant hate-filled arguments with my father. It is hardly surprising that my mother became seriously ill with breast cancer and only narrowly escaped death. This illness was for my mother like a twist of fate. She knew that she had to fight not only for her physical survival, but had to accomplish the exit from the self-built prisons of marriage and psychoanalysis; it was all now a question of survival.

Her health was restored and she got a divorce in 1974. She began to free herself in decisive steps. She transformed her whole life, enjoying her independence. She truly came to life, left everything and everyone connected with her old life behind. That included me. She made it unmistakably clear to me that she finally wanted to live her own life. After she had almost persecuted me with her attention in my youth (see Chapter VIII), I now witnessed only from a distance what she did. This situation lasted from 1974 until 1976. This time saw her renewed interest in Judaism, and included various trips to Israel. In Tel Aviv, she visited her cousin Eva, the daughter of Fishel England, and Eva's husband.

She took painting classes and became fully absorbed in her newfound passion. Only later, during the research for this book, did I find out that she also had reestablished contact with her cousins in Paris and America.

We only got closer again in 1975, after she settled into a spacious apartment in Zollikerberg, a rural area outside of Zurich. The move away from the city, from the beautiful apartment, was for my mother a hugely painful parting. She realized that a long and significant phase of life had come to an end, and that she was about to begin a brand-new life, alone and on her own. She worked mainly at home as a psychoanalyst and supervisor and dedicated herself to her passions: psychological science and painting.

As a result of her radical life change, my mother opened a new battlefront: psychoanalysis. The rebellious child from former times reawakened. She asked questions as she used to and provoked her colleagues whenever she could. Her intelligence was fully on display. She did not hide any longer behind a facade, a mask, but sought open confrontation: she dared to write down her thoughts in a noteworthy article. The provocation culminated in the attempt to publish an independent article in the official body of psychoanalysis, the journal *Psyche*: "Depression and Grandiosity as Related Expressions of the Narcissistic Disturbances" (1978). The article was rejected as unscientific and below the standards of psychoanalysis and turned down by the editors. The readers did not get the opportunity to form their own opinion about new thoughts within the psychoanalytical society. The whole orientation of this publication was aimed at guarding psychoanalysis against an "impure" body of thought. But my mother could not be thwarted; after all, she was used to getting her way and asserting her opinion. Without further ado she dared to take the step into independence and expanded the essay into a book: *The Drama of the Gifted Child* (1979).

THE HAPPINESS OF
WRITING—THE DRAMA OF
THE GIFTED CHILD

Writing became her life perspective, it brought liberation from life-long adaptation. Finally she could let her thoughts run free. In a bold move she wrote her first book, *The Drama of a Gifted Child*. At 28, I became a witness to this process. It was the time when my mother and I were closest. My mother shared her thoughts with me, and I came to know her as a completely different person: passionate, open, approachable, relaxed. She changed radically—it was as if she were virtually merging with her thoughts, as if body and spirit found one another. For the first time I could sense that my mother felt happy. All of it was real. The book was indeed her own history. This is why this book was and is so authentic.

For my mother, writing this book must have been nothing less than the exit from her false self. Nothing and no one could silence her anymore; she no longer pretended, did not disavow what she deemed right. The book is autobiographical, even though she does not lift the veil. She describes how people suffer when they have to adapt to the outside world and deny themselves in order to survive. She describes the extraordinary talent of human beings to conform, if they must, for the sake of their existence. But she does not leave it at that: she analyzes this adaptability, which was (and is) socially approved, and unmasks it as a fatal consequence of parental upbringing. She describes how children adapt to their parents' emotional needs, how parents project their unmet emotional needs onto their children and rob them of the chance to develop their own originality, to feel their own feelings. Accordingly, she understands mental disorders as a consequence of emotional self-alienation: grandiose and narcissistic behavior, and depression, are the consequences. In grandiosity, the lurking depression is warded off. Depression is the expression of the true self being blocked from developing in a sympathetic, nurturing social environment.

My mother had her finger firmly on the pulse of those times. For the first time, a psychological author dared to attack parents head-on in their conduct in raising their children. She did this by radically introducing the perspective of the child into psychology. The emotional exploitation of children by their parents was denounced, and parents were held responsible for the widespread mental disorders of society: every child, my mother demanded, has the right to develop his or her originality.

At the same time she revolutionized the psychotherapeutic way of working. Those undergoing therapy had a right to find out about how their parents had behaved towards them. The objective of therapy was to find out this truth for oneself, and to claim the right to develop one's own true self. Adults do not have to remain in a state of dependence and compliance towards their parents, but have the right to develop their potential autonomously.

These are the concepts of *The Drama of the Gifted Child* in the year 1979. And then a miracle happened: the book became a bestseller and Alice Miller a star.

My mother's success was like a wildfire. Her book became an international bestseller, was translated into 30 languages— a triumph. But the more famous my mother became, the more she struggled with the public's perception of her. She felt persecuted and old fears made their presence felt once again. The public became threatening. It was her greatest concern that her private life could be made public, that her life history would become known. She became increasingly paranoid. Today it is clear to me that her war experiences gradually took control, and that my mother, on an unconscious level, could not distinguish the old experience of the war and present reality—they had the same taste.

During this time we maintained our mutually trusting relationship. I suspect that she found protection and comfort in our interactions during those turbulent times. Once again, she made me her confidant in the preparation of her next book. *For Your Own Good* (1980) was a sequel to her first book. Here she addressed in particular the destructive pedagogical mechanisms of "Black Pedagogy," ("Poisonous Pedagogy" in the English translation) a concept created by Katharina Rutschky (1941–2010). Once again, the book was an instant success. My mother made connections between the popular pedagogical ideology and self-denial, and analyzed repressive upbringing as the cause of psychological suffering. Her theme was the psychodynamic of destructive child-rearing mechanisms.

My mother outlined most perceptively how a child-rearing ideology established itself in the course of history. Specifically, in the development of parent-child relationships, parents ask more and more how they may "gain control" over their children; my mother revealed these pedagogical mechanisms as a pure instrument of power. In the course of history, the child becomes the parents' enemy, against whom the parents have to fight by means of child-rearing. "Poisonous Pedagogy" had always worked towards inventing new methods of pedagogical terror to limit the aliveness of the child. My mother criticized this sharply and demonstrated how these child-rearing experiences lead to neurotic disturbances in the adult. To support her theory, my mother traced the histories of Adolf Hitler, the drug addict Christiane F., and the serial killer Jürgen Bartsch. She showed how the effects of people's child-rearing experiences are acted out later in life as a behavior pattern against themselves or others, due to the destructive pedagogical mechanisms they endured.

At the end of the book, she pointed out that it was imperative for clients to address and process in psychotherapy the destructive behavior patterns of their parents. Thus she broke completely new ground in psychotherapy. This topic would grip my mother during her whole career as a writer.

Her third book, *Thou Shalt Not Be Aware* (1981), addresses disease-inducing behavior of human beings, who may not be aware of their own suffering as being caused by their parents. The title poses a commandment from the parents, who are indeed the origin of the suffering, and who have, as the perpetrators, a vested interest that their children, the victims, never become aware of what was done to them. Here, Alice Miller formulates her psychotherapeutic vision: the goal of therapy is for the patients to find their own "truth," understand their own biography, and clearly identify their parents' misdeeds. In this process, the therapist is the enlightened witness who supports the patient in these efforts. When patients can realize and mourn the repressed pain of their tortured childhoods, they become free, and can live their own true selves and realize their full potential.

What made my mother's theoretical approach special: it was developed radically from the child's perspective. Adults usually write from their own point of view about children, but have difficulty empathizing with the emotional state of the child. Alice Miller saw herself as the advocate of the child and, for the first time, gave voice to children in their relationship with their parents. She stood vehemently against the common view that the therapist has to get across to clients, in lengthy therapy sessions, the need to adopt a forgiving attitude toward parental misconduct. On the contrary, Alice was convinced that clients have the right in therapy to confront their own history of suffering and those who caused it; to liberate themselves, with the loyal support of the therapist, from persistent heteronomy; to discover their own potential and at last fulfill it in real life.

She was driven during those years. On the one hand was her burgeoning fame, which for her remained a matter of ambivalence, and the commercial side of her success. On the other hand, there was the uncanny urge to articulate her ideas, which she had stifled for decades. She had a downright limitless sense of mission. It was during this time that she became a committed adversary against her former family, psychoanalysis. By branding Sigmund Freud's turning away from his seduction theory towards his theory of the Oedipus complex as untruthful and cowardly, she threw down the gauntlet to the psychoanalysts. She reproached them for leaving patients in ignorance, and for manipulating analysands during therapy to forgive their parents and abandon the child's perspective. From her perspective, analysands were thereby urged to suppress their own history of suffering and remain forever confined to their prisons.

Because of this criticism she fell out for good with her former psychoanalytical colleagues and friends in Zurich. Once more I wish to quote Alexander Moser:

> Your mother was for years an important member in our discussion circle. We all benefitted from her creative and profound contributions. Also she herself felt very comfortable in our group. But the success of her books changed her very much. Increasingly, she experienced friendly and well-meaning criticism no longer as positively stimulating, but as an obstacle and hindrance to the further development of her own ideas. So she withdrew, to our regret, more and more and eventually broke off contact completely.

Of course, my mother saw it all quite differently. After the publication of her first book, she had already given up her psychoanalytic practice and her teaching at the seminary; in 1988, she finally resigned from the Swiss Society for Psychoanalysis and devoted herself fully to the fight against "Poisonous Pedagogy."

With her first three books, Alice Miller had created her own, free world. As an author, she stepped into the open, in literal as well as figurative terms, since her books were rarely created at the writing desk. With a Dictaphone, she took extensive walks in the forest and thus developed and recorded her thoughts. When she later lived in the south of France, she gravitated towards a small mountain lake outside of Saint Rémy de Provence, where she composed most of her books under an open sky. Writing assistants then typed the text from the Dictaphone, which she herself in turn edited. Maybe this is why her texts appear so fresh and spontaneous. When reading her books, one never feels the exertion of a writer laboring to set down thoughts. Her texts are light as a feather. The difference between her personal life and her life as an author is striking: in her writing world she was casual, spontaneous, uncomplicated, hopeful, self-confident, tolerant and often joyous, but also without fear and willing to fight. In her daily life she was suspicious, frightened, tense, aggressive, withholding, very complicated, unreliable, increasingly narcissistic, and insensitive. In her books she asserted an argumentative logic of the highest level and had no need to aggressively insult other people. In her everyday life, I observed how my mother embroiled herself in disputes with other people. The divorce war with my father was by no means my mother's only battlefield.

For a long time, I have been appalled and incensed by this contrast—the degree to which my mother's personal life directly contradicted her own insights. I am her son and was assuredly not her therapist. The way my mother behaved toward me remains as well a very painful issue. In her theoretical world, the helpless child is given a prominent place and receives unique attention. Needless to say, her theory derived from her own negative experiences with her parents, who did not provide the support she needed. She felt unseen, misunderstood, and abandoned. That she then repeated with me, her own child, this parental behavior, which had so hurt and burdened her, may also have played a role in the development of her theories. Later, she would find ways, again and again, to reaffirm how sorry she was about how badly she had treated me in my childhood.

Unfortunately, these insights had no effect on improving our relationship—quite the contrary. Her everyday actions did not change. Only at the end of the 1990s, after grueling battles, did she recognize sadly, albeit only partially, the extent of her guilt in what had transpired.

VARIATIONS OF A LIFE THEME— ALICE MILLER'S WAR AGAINST PARENTS

"The fourth commandment, supported by traditional morality, demands of us to honor and love our parents so that—thus goes the hidden threat—we may live a long life. This commandment of honoring out of fear demands universal validity. Those who want to follow it, even though they were disrespected, mistreated, misused by their parents, can only do this if they deny their true emotions. The body often rebels against this denial and this ignoring of unresolved childhood traumas with severe illnesses. (German blurb to *Die Revolte des Körpers*, 2004—*The Body Never Lies*.)

My mother remained faithful to her themes. In her late works, Alice Miller evermore pointed to the somatic dangers brought about by the denial of one's own history. This denial not only refers to the facts of the biography, but above all to the emotions being suppressed. It is now known from neurobiology that every experience we have in relation to reality, to the outside world, is emotionally represented and stored in the body. As my mother was not overly familiar with the newest research results of neurobiology, her later theoretical treatises were partially quite speculative. Still, she had a good nose for current issues.

Only today do we know how humans experience emotions; specifically, that emotions are primarily biological phenomena which unconsciously ensure for us communication between the nerve cells and the brain. Emotions are quite simply the language of the brain. Without emotional information from the organism, the brain is helpless and cannot react. Without emotions, we are not at all able to survive.

Today, one can hardly claim any longer that emotions can be easily suppressed—and that this is a good thing. We certainly try to get a grip on our feelings, or we fend them off as best as we can. In principle we need, children need, an emotional, mental world which enables them to perceive their feelings in the first place. We only develop this emotional, mental world through a benevolent, empathic social environment. As infants are being mirrored by a caregiver, they can gradually develop access to their feelings, which, as Antonio Damasio has described in his books, are the intellectual (mental) representation of biological processes.

These findings of developmental psychology and neurobiology have lasting consequences for psychotherapy: by mirroring, the therapist has to give clients the experience of first discovering and developing their mental world of feelings. Only then are clients able to emotionally reconstruct their history. By combining the knowledge (of biographical facts) with the feelings belonging to them, a new connection arises which makes it possible for clients to understand their own history in the spirit of Alice Miller. Then therapy has created the conditions to get out of the hurtful and life-hindering false parts of the self.

The therapist helps clients form a consciousness of their own history by disclosing coherences. Thanks to this knowledge, patients find entirely new pathways to implement their resources and needs autonomously and as adults. They can protect themselves from manipulation and heteronomy because they are no longer the helpless victims of parental programming from the past. Detached from parental influence, clients can begin to live their own lives.

Alice Miller believed that the lives of children would have taken a different course if they had not been at their parents' mercy; if there had been, for example, another adult, an enlightened witness, standing by their side. But because of isolation, children have no choice but to adapt themselves to the parents. They develop a false self, and the eventual consequences are psychic and somatic illnesses. An enlightened witness might have been able to intervene. But Alice Miller was aware that this idea was usually nothing but a beautiful dream. Even today, there is insufficient willingness to hold parents accountable for their failed conduct. This is why Alice demanded that the therapist must assume the role of enlightened witness. Therapists, she argued, are tasked to put themselves at the service of the client. They may not spare the parents and should support their clients, using every effort, in the investigation of their history, precisely as enlightened witnesses. As loyalty towards parents is still deeply rooted in society, this demand was unusual and very radical—both then and now.

VIII. Inherited Suffering— The Mother

THE SILENT WITNESS—MY CHILDHOOD AND YOUTH 1950–1972

When I am asked about childhood memories, one incident comes to the foreground with striking persistence. It is not in itself spectacular, it does not represent any of the various violent experiences, which I suffered, but its aura is so present within me that I have come to comprehend it as a defining moment in establishing my role in the family.

I must have been about eight years old. My parents earned extra income by correcting galley proofs for a publisher. I remember how my parents sat in intense concentration at the dining table. I watched them. Keeping silent. For hours, so it seems to me. I did not really understand what they were doing, but it was clear that I was not to make any noise. Absolute silence reigned. And this great silence enveloped my parents and me, as it were, from the beginning. We had no common language. My isolation increased because my parents usually spoke Polish with one another, while I only learned German, and Swiss German at that. My parents never entertained the idea to consider and self-criticize their behavior towards me. They made me an outsider within the family. As a child, I could not make sense of this behavior and simply did not understand why I was so excluded from my own family. Only later did I understand that parents tend to project their own burdens onto their children. Later, I realized with horror that I had become a foreigner in my parents' family, just as my parents had been foreigners in Switzerland. Both were so busy trying to put the war behind them and regain their foothold in society at long last that the needs of a child were simply secondary.

I became the silent observer of my parents, and this great silence surrounded for decades all that happened to me: the disregard, the emotional assaults, the lack of interest in me as a person, even into adulthood. My outsider status caused me to interact with my family in a complex way. Because of my role as observer, I was forced to keenly monitor my environment. I developed a kind of x-ray vision, virtually absorbing all movements and remarks. I absolutely wanted to understand what was happening around me. Nobody explained to me what was going on, so I had to make reality accessible for myself solely through observing. This method runs the significant risk of error. I am glad to say that I did not become psychotic, but instead I developed a great skill, a sensitivity for grasping human behavior. It comes naturally to me to read and understand non-verbal communication between people. As a therapist, this ability has helped me time and again to detect and understand complicated psychic correlations.

Incidentally, as an adult, during the 1990s, I experienced a culmination of the assaults from my mother when I was in a severe crisis after the separation from my first wife. At my mother's urging, I underwent primal therapy with a woman student of Konrad Stettbacher, who at that time my mother still enthusiastically promoted. That I could later unmask this man as a fraud can be traced back to my competence as a silent observer. I shall return to this point.

Today I know of course that parents, who have borne the heavy burdens of war, persecution, flight, migration, and economic hardship, have great difficulty feeling empathy with the world of their children. Even knowing this, it is nevertheless hard for me to read my experiences against this background. As a therapist, I can do so; as a son, it still is painful, even decades later. The situation is even more difficult as the son of Alice Miller, world-famous researcher on childhood, who has fought like no other for the rights of children to their own psychic development and against physically abusive parents.

But let's start at the beginning: I was born in April of 1950, while both my parents were writing their dissertations. When I was an adult, Alice Miller once described to me how traumatic birth and the months after had been for her. I quote from memory:

> When the contractions began, I went to the Zurich cantonal hospital. I was terribly afraid of giving birth. On the birthing bed, I was seized by a huge panic, old fears surfaced. I felt totally helpless, and in this situation, the contractions suddenly stopped. It took three long days before I could start another attempt to give birth to you. During those days, I walked around on the hill of Mount Zurich, racked with immense guilt feelings and fears to have failed as a mother. I felt all alone with my fate. No one supported me, not even your father. Finally, the contractions began again, and you were born healthy.

This time, the birth was without problems, but you were scarcely born when the first difficulties began: I felt completely overwhelmed dealing with you, a helpless child, and you did not exactly make it easy for me to take my first steps as a mother. From the beginning, you refused to feed at the breast. I was very offended. I was so disappointed that my own child rejected me and my motherly love. I had to let milk be pumped and you drank in very small doses.

It must have been enormously difficult for my mother that I, a baby, was "controlling" her whole daily routine, needing her full attention and practically "dictating" through my physical needs how she had to live her life. In any case, she could not cope with it. It was pure horror for my mother to have someone else dictate to her what to do. I cannot remember one single incident where my mother allowed me my self-initiative. On the contrary, self-initiative was systematically prohibited. She admitted this later, and frequently talked about heavy guilt feelings. Officially, my mother always told me the following version when she explained the reasons why she had handed me off to an acquaintance shortly after birth: "Because your father and I were so busy with our dissertations and the living space was too small, we felt we could not raise a child while in this situation, so we had to give you away."

Based on my research, and the knowledge I have gained from writing this book, I would today no longer deem this version as valid. That I had refused breast milk struck my mother emotionally to the heart. This early relationship experience is, in my opinion, one of the reasons why our relationship was burdened for all these years. Later, I will recount some more incidents that support this thesis.

This acquaintance clearly had no ability with newborns. I am said to have stayed with her for two weeks, crying and screaming a lot and having been in a very poor condition, until aunt Ala took me in. Irenka told me, "If we had not fetched you, you would have died." I spent the first half year of my life with Ala, Bunio, and Irenka, who then was eighteen years old. My parents remained strangers for me.

The next major rupture was the birth of my sister Julika in 1956. She was born, as said before, with Down syndrome. Her birth, and the fact that my father had hidden from my mother that his sister had had this disability, plunged my parents' marriage into further deepening crisis. Ironically this child was supposed to save the dysfunctional marriage of my parents. But the gap between the two of them only widened. We children were given away. Julika returned to my parents after just one year. I stayed for two years in a children's home on the Au peninsula. I was told that this was necessary to cure me of bedwetting. During this time, I basically had no contact with my family. I completely forgot that I had a sister. Nevertheless, I don't have bad memories of this time with "Aunt Alice," as we called the director of the children's home. Only my enrollment in school turned into a disaster. No one had prepared me for school, I did not get on well, felt lost and overwhelmed, especially with the demands of school. From then on, school always remained a difficult topic, and my unsatisfactory performance became a favorite theme of fatherly contempt.

As I had been taken unexpectedly to the children's home, I was just as unexpectedly picked up. I was eight years old. My parents had since moved. Everything seemed new and strange to me after my two-year absence. In the big living room hung a swing from the ceiling where a little girl was sitting with an odd facial expression—my sister.

I did not like her, and my antipathy was inflamed rather than dampened by my parents' behavior, as they expected constant consideration from me. Our maids or nannies remained my major attachment figures during the following years. Together with them, I formed a family within the family; I spoke German with them, while my parents spoke Polish with one another. However, the domestic help changed often; my mother probably found it hard to tolerate that her son was closer to his nannies than to her.

My father was as cruel and violent as he could be charming and winning. Outings with him often concluded with me being sick from exhaustion. It seems he wanted to make me into a "real man." He could be endearing, cook my favorite meal, and then again, completely out of nowhere, hit me. I loved him—as a child loves his father—and had an unspeakable fear of him because he remained unpredictable in his moods and attacks. How much I was afraid of him became clear to me only years later in the context of therapy. He tortured me in many ways—emotionally and physically. My mother, who herself was in a permanent war with him, allowed him to have his way. During this time, she had totally disappeared into her psychoanalytic world, was often not at home, and when at home was usually preoccupied.

When we moved in 1960 from Rapperswil to Zurich, she soon had her treatment room adjoining wall to wall with our apartment. We had to be quiet all the time, because she was always tired or on the move. It was impossible to reach out to her; she alone decided when she had time and interest. I did not have the impression that my experiences were of interest to my parents. Emotionally, I was left to myself.

Only when I was seventeen and spending the last years of high school in a Catholic boarding school, did my mother excessively intensify contact with me by telephone. It had been my wish to go to the boarding school. I felt much freer there than at home, even though the management of the school was strict. But it was so much more comfortable than the oppressive-aggressive atmosphere at home. At any rate, an odd relationship by telephone developed with my mother. She called every day, always during mealtime. While my peers were eating, I was called to the telephone. And every Sunday, I had to speak with her on the phone for at least an hour. I cannot recall ever standing up for myself against this massive harassment. On the one hand, I probably did not dare to, and on the other hand, I finally felt respected and noticed.

After the end of high-school I would have liked to study at the university. But my parents did not think me capable. I trained to become an elementary teacher and soon stood on my own two feet. Childhood was over.

ALICE—DISCIPLE OF KONRAD STETTBACHER— AND THE PERSECUTED SON, 1983–1994

Allow me a leap in time of more than ten years. I have already shared that my mother and I had a wonderful phase of good contact while she was writing her first three books. In 1980 I began to study psychology. Already while I was working as a teacher, I had attended seminars in the Psychoanalytic Seminar; the exchanges with my mother about *The Drama of the Gifted Child* had fascinated me. Now I wanted to find my own path as a therapist. Even though my mother welcomed my desire to become a therapist, and had explicitly encouraged me, she thought nothing of me attending university. Nor did she take seriously my therapeutic teachers Jan Bastiaans (Leiden) or Christel Schöttler (Gießen). As I see it today, my mother could not bear that I struck out on my own. I was escaping her control.

Instead, in 1983 she suggested that I undergo primal therapy with Konrad Stettbacher (1930–2016) whom she had by then discovered and by whose methods she swore. However, "suggested" is putting it mildly. Without consulting me—I was, after all, thirty-three-years old—she had reserved a place for me in his therapy practice. Out of the blue, I received in September of 1983 a letter from Stettbacher, in which he asked me to transfer a five-figure sum to reserve a place with him for 1985. I was appalled, refused, and confronted my mother. She had an unprecedented angry outburst: I was crazy to refuse the offer. This would be the only way for me. She only wanted to help me. Finally, she had found a way to make up for her mistakes of the past. How dare I reject the offer, etc. Our relationship deteriorated dramatically. She experienced my refusal, as I see it today, as a declaration of war, as a threatening loss of control. The above-mentioned scene of breast-feeding was repeating itself. Once again, I had refused mother's breast. We were in a permanent feud, she criticized my first wife, my weight, my non-relationship with Julika, she denigrated my therapeutic teachers.... The letter of 1987, documented at the beginning of this book, needs to be read also against this backdrop.

Over and over again, she harangued me, until finally, in 1992, because of a severe personal crisis I effectively gave in. My first marriage had failed, I was emotionally and financially drained. In this situation, my mother repeated her suggestion. She placed me with a student of Stettbacher in Munich. Once again, my mother and I had intense exchanges, at times daily faxes went back and forth. I had to write a biography for the therapy, which included information about my parents. In those days she talked to me for the first time about the war.

What I did not know: my therapist sent the recordings of our sessions to Stettbacher; he reported to my mother, and she in turn tried to influence me in her letters in line with her own interests. She was convinced that she knew what was wrong with me and how best to help me. And she reacted more and more aggressively—as I see it today—the more I defied this exertion of influence, her sovereignty of interpretation.

At first, though, she strongly encouraged me to confront her with her failure—in a communication dated April 27, 1992, for instance, she wrote, "I am so glad that you can show me your mistrust and also tell me about it." She talked a lot about her guilt feelings, and how delighted she was that I, by undergoing the Stettbacher therapy, was on a path toward resolution. I felt more and more uncomfortable because of this persecuting motherly attention and realized with horror that her role in my therapeutic process was entirely counterproductive. She made many suggestions and demanded "complete information": "I must be allowed to ask you until I see the situation sufficiently complete, in order to understand your actions." Above all, she was driven by the idea that I was protecting my father, so that I could attack her unhindered, indeed that I was becoming more and more like him.

At the beginning of 1993, I reached a point in the therapy—still unaware that my mother was unofficially "supervising" it—when I asked her for more restraint:

> I would like to ask you, even though you mean well, to trust me that am working in my therapy. I have felt very pushed by your interventions and ask you to give me my space. ... In this process, I ask you not to crush me with your ardor and not to disturb me. For sure, I now need some time to grapple for myself with my parents. I will get in touch by phone when I feel emotionally capable. Because I cannot confront things and be nice at the same time. I suppress

something. But it is so difficult for a child to observe, against his own nature, realities which are unthinkable for him, which should not be. I am exactly at this point now. It hurts so much, makes me so angry. I need space to process this. (February 4, 1993)

My mother could not give me this space. When I read today the letters she wrote me during the 1980s and 1990s, when I was in my late thirties and forties, I can hardly believe what I am reading. They are always evidence of a dreadful lack of respect for my boundaries. After her failure in my childhood, she now wanted to be my therapist. She wanted to show me the way. As long as I followed her suggestions, she remained warmhearted and accommodating. But when I began to distance myself, and wanted to know, for example, how she had experienced my father's role in my childhood, she totally shut down. On January 6, 1994, I wrote to her:

I have already told you several times how my father forced me every morning, for years, to wash myself with him. You were always lying down in the room next door and yet were so far away from me. Already then, I suffered horribly from this. But I never dared to say anything. Today, I could scream because of this humiliation. During my adolescence, I was constantly subjected to a controlling invasion of my privacy. Still today, I feel defenseless. ... I am convinced that this whole thing was sexual abuse, only very disguised. Did you then notice anything? Did this washing procedure never puzzle you?

Were you afraid to protect me from my father, when he contrived tasks that were torturous? What were you thinking, then, when he laughed at me every lunchtime at the table and cut me short? How did you feel when I always had to concede everything to Julika? Did you feel sorry for me? Do you now understand why I could not believe all your statements about my father? *[In the context of the divorce, she had told me horrible stories about him—MM.]* Should I have believed you when I was always alone during those days, though under your eyes, at the mercy of this man? ... I would like to talk with you about these questions because the feeling that I was handed over to this man by you burdens both me and our relationship very much. That is to say I am becoming conscious that I have vegetated my whole life in a prison of loneliness. Today, I want to undertake everything to free myself from this prison. With these conversations, you can help me in this work and support me.

She did not respond. On the contrary, she fought back and accused me of blaming her for the deeds of my father, in order to protect him. We had severe, completely fruitless confrontations. Her tone with me became ice cold. An example:

Martin, I asked you on Monday if you are still of the opinion that I was "perfidiously manipulating" you and giving you "dishonest advice"—the opinion that you conclusively expressed about me in your letter of August 1993. You told me (and you showed me clearly) that this question of mine made you angry. You wanted to look at this for yourself and call me, when you have come to a clear conclusion. But you did not call anymore. Meanwhile the scales fell from my eyes. I have had to fully realize that your "therapy" is a mere fiction, a beautiful illusion and self-deception—nothing more. ... You attack me constantly because of my culpability in your childhood, which I have acknowledged and apologized for to you in detail several times. Time and again, you try to capitalize on that. In your zeal you even go so far as to blame me for things which definitively your father committed. ... It is your decision. You have received everything from me to help you and to become healthy. But you obviously did not want it. ... Instead of doing everything to become healthy, you cultivate your blindness (for example toward me) and thus destroy yourself more and more. (January 6, 1994)

Also here I discover a repetition of the initial primal scene: I do not want to accept the sustenance of my mother.

The situation escalated in such a way that my mother tried to eliminate me professionally as a therapist based on Stettbacher's slanderous attempts to thwart my career. He had led my mother to believe—a letter to that effect is in my files—that I was a danger to my patients, that I was infantile and mean, and was capitalizing on my mother's name. My mother believed this man blindly. Hereafter, she exerted incredible pressure on me. It was a time of persecution. I received threatening letters, she alleged that I lied, she accused me of failure and worse. I began to doubt myself, was completely beside myself, on the brink of suicide.

Only when I confronted her in 1994 with the results of my inquiries regarding Stettbacher, who had absolutely no therapeutic qualifications, did she give in. Because of this I had travelled specifically and spontaneously to Provence. Our relationship never recovered from this conversation where I could prove to her, point by point, that she had been deceived by a fraudster, and that, because of her promotion of him, she had endangered not only my life, but also the lives of countless other humans, who trusted her advice.

I sued Stettbacher in the fall of 1994 and I won my case. The public dissociation of my mother from him, after years of advocating for him, is known. She distanced herself in big newspaper interviews. She wrote to me on October 1, 1994:

> Dear Martin, you have told me that you will sue Konrad Stettbacher in court because of infringement of your personal rights. I can understand your decision well because now I know that these violations had devastating, grave consequences for your professional existence and your life, as they drove you to the brink of suicide.
>
> It was they *[Stettbacher and his assistant]* who caused your therapist *[this female assistant of Stettbacher]*, to threaten you with the termination of therapy unless you gave up your long-standing practice right away. And they prompted me to threaten you with a public dissociation of your activity, unless you follow their ultimatum to stop seeing clients.
>
> My actions towards you were based on the communication of Mister Stettbacher that more than eight people had told him of your criminal deeds. When I asked him in my horror for details, I always received only the information that he could not tell me any details because his information came from clients and he could not violate professional confidence.

Why I believed this information, which I myself could not verify, has several reasons, which I figured out after long research. But the fact is that I acted out of this belief, and for this, I bear, and will bear, full responsibility. ...

Although it was Stettbacher's false information that led me to put you under pressure (because then I wanted to do everything so that your therapy would not be terminated), I committed these acts as an adult on my own responsibility. For this, I will and must make a formal apology to you. I am very sorry that I did not see any possibility at that time to check with you if the information of Mister Stettbacher was even true.—Your mother

During the years that followed, our contact remained encumbered. She acted as though her apology and disso-ciation from Stettbacher had taken the whole story off the table. But I was just beginning to work through this har-rowing experience with my mother. More and more I real-ized how much I had been traumatized by this experience of persecution. I experienced myself as the victim of a tre-mendous brainwashing. Looking through the letters, which I received from my mother during the years of therapy, it once again became clear how it was systematically ham-mered into me that I was the victim of false perceptions, and that virtually an internalized devil in the person of my father spoke through me. She accused me of being a mon-ster and completely disturbed.

Even though I was proven right, I neither could feel joy nor satisfaction that I was not in the wrong. Rather, I still had to deal for years with the consequences of this disastrous therapy experience and the acting out of my mother. Above all, Hugo Stamm's book *Sects: Under the Spell of Addiction and Power; Help for Affected Persons and Relatives to Get Out* (1995) helped me process and classify my experiences of the previous twelve years. Those experiences, I discovered, were akin to those of a typical victim of a destructive psycho-sect. On the basis of these realizations it became harder and harder for me to take my mother seriously as an expert on therapy. I still appreciate her first three books, whose basic assumptions are immensely valuable and blazed a trail for a new way of thinking. But I could not (and cannot) grant her more. When she approached me with an extensive confession in 1998—it will be documented below—it was of little use to me. Even though I tried initially to build an objective and respectful relationship—it pretty much failed. And during these years, it was not important to me. I was living in a happy relationship, I was involved in reordering my life, and I wanted nothing to do with the old stories any more. I decided to "freeze" the relationship with her and to be available only in an emergency.

LETTER OF MY MOTHER OF
MAY 28, 1998

D^{ear Martin,}

Recently, I have once again read through your letters of the last years and then my reactions to them, and it struck me how much I reject and fight off what you accuse me of, out of fear you could be right. But you are right. Howsoever a human being experiences and feels his mother—she has given him reasons. For a long time, I refused to believe that this sentence also applies to our relationship, tried to lay the blame on your father, but it does not work. You have not only suffered in your childhood and youth because of me, but you were driven to the last brink of despair because of the therapy with E. and the manipulations of the guru. And I cannot deny that I myself personally drove you into this misery. That I meant well does not change anything about the facts that it was poison. For a long time, I could not admit it fully because it is so monstrous; it is so horrible that I did not in the least sense the dangers resulting from it.

You told me in Zurich in the car what state you were driven into in Munich [the place of the therapy—MM] *and I was so frightened that I probably had to ward off this fear. I did not want to recognize my guilt because it was so huge. During the following weeks I had the impression that I could not reach you; that is why I avoided your visit, when in fact it was I who had made herself*

131

unreachable. Now I see it much more clearly. I was afraid of your reproaches because I was afraid of the weight of the guilt towards you, which I did not want to own. Now I have to do it. For such a long time, I did not want to acknowledge that I was obviously for you the mother that you show to me. I called your accounts lies or smiled at them, tried to bend your perceptions in order to look better. But there are no means to undo what has happened. Everything that you have experienced with me belongs to your truth, and I don't have the right to correct anything in it, just because your image of me is so hard for me to bear: a persecuting, possessive, hate-filled, dangerous, destructive mother—I never wanted to be all that. Therefore I defended myself. But my letters, which you present to me, where you point out the violations, only show the facts. These are attacks on your integrity. I can no longer deny this.

Before I die, I wanted to tell this to you. If I had been a reasonably good mother for you, you would never have such a bad image of me. Therefore I was the way you see me. This is quite logical for me. I can no longer cast off, or sidestep, this truth. No longer will I evade my son because now I am no longer afraid of him. He only told me the truth, which I did not want to hear. But I no longer want to flee from it.

I have abandoned you so often during your childhood, left you with other people, did not understand properly your needs, fears and despair, and instead of empathizing with you, I sent you to aunt Ala. Instead of understanding you, because I could not, I drove you into a therapy that not only was of no use to you but endangered your life. I should have actually grasped this when I saw the photo of you at your place, your weight and your face full of despair. Instead of finally confronting myself with this, I tried to tell you two weeks later over the telephone that you were doing better than ever before. Yes, but despite of the therapy, not because of it. You have only yourself to thank for the individual steps of healing from bulimia, from the lack of ability to relate to others, and from your blindness towards your mother.

Also my letter to Manuela [my life companion—MM] was driven by fear and denial. I was not yet ready for an encounter because I could not process so quickly what you had told me in Zurich about Munich, nor the statement of the photos, could also not yet admit that you were right. It is a great insult to learn from your own child how heartlessly, blindly and stupidly one treated one's own child. One wants to forget it and have it forgiven. But wherefrom should a child practice charity to people who have harmed him in life-threatening ways, and on top of it want to force him to forget?

I was able to empathize with many people, but only with my son I could not. When he told me, I denied it. I? Is there not evidence that others felt understood by me? And this should not be possible for me where it was so important to me? Where I strove so hard? Yes, it was just like this. <u>Especially with him I lacked empathy</u>. Not without reason. If I had been capable of empathy for his situation, then I would have had to recognize myself in the way I was <u>toward him</u>: unaware, cold, harsh, critical, over-correcting, disciplinarian, and never truly as I wanted to be, as I imagined myself to be. This false ideal of myself I even imposed on him and thus confused his perceptions. When he no longer allowed himself to be confused, I finally had to look in the mirror. I had to see that I had treated my first child almost like my mother had treated me. Despite my training I did not succeed in escaping this fate. Now at least I no longer want to deny it. On his first day of school, I did not accompany him to school and thought nothing of it. It did not occur to me to drive to the Au. How was this possible? I don't know. Only when he told me what this meant for him did I begin to comprehend. But I continued wanting to dissuade myself and him of the truth, so that I would not suffer, so that I would not have to bear the comparison with my mother. Now there is no escape. Now I am also old enough to bear the truth and to no longer run away from it. Why? A ruined life cannot be polished up with lies. Neither a lost motherhood.

THE SON AS PERSECUTOR—THE POWER OF THE WAR TRAUMA

While writing this book, I also established contact with a former friend of my mother, the therapist Barbara Rogers. She lives in Mexico today and worked closely together with my mother between 1999 and 2007. She also was a kind of therapeutic companion for my mother—even if only by telephone. But after a conflict, my mother cut off contact with her as well. When I asked Ms. Rogers if my mother had ever talked about me in connection with the Stettbacher crisis, she was astonished: "Your mother never mentioned you. Now, when you ask me, it strikes me that your mother kept silent about you. Actually, you did not exist at all. And if ever, she talked very badly about you. Basically, your mother refused to talk about her experiences with Stettbacher. So I did not dare any longer to touch upon the background of this story."

Barbara Rogers was not an isolated case. After the death of my mother, in various conversations with other people, I had to take note of the fact that after this shameful and embarrassing incident, my mother had simply erased my existence. In her public discourse, I had become a non-person.

It is difficult to put into words how much this fact, which Ms. Rogers summed up in a nutshell, has vexed me. Even my mother's seemingly well-intentioned letter of May 1998 essentially lost its value. I felt lied to. What did this two-faced pattern of communication pattern amount to? To me, she made an admission of guilt; with her therapeutic friend, I became an object of silence or insult.

At first, I could not make any sense at all of this contradictory behavior of my mother, but during the past months, in tandem with my research, I have developed a theory which seems plausible to me: the drama around Stettbacher, at the outset, turned on my mother's disappointment that I was not acceding to her wishes and expectations. Indeed, initially I did not want to undergo therapy with her guru, which she experienced as an incredible catastrophe. She had an unprecedented outburst. At the time, I found her simply hysterical; today I suspect that my "no" must have triggered suppressed feelings in my mother, which belong in the context of the war trauma that she never processed. I became the victim of a projection against which I had no defense.

Her recommendation to undergo therapy with Stettbacher, or better, the precise motives that led to this behavior, were not clear to me then and until recently. I can remember well how I never felt perceived at all by my mother in this context. It was as if she were talking not to me, but to someone else. But I was struck, time and again, by the emotional fervor with which she advised me to undertake this step—as if it were a matter of life and death—and how deeply hurt she was when I rejected her "help," providing a clear justification for my position. The more I refused, the more aggressive my mother became.

Today I think that for her it really was a matter of life and death, and she actually was speaking to a different person—her father. Therefore, I see today in this story not only a morally revolting and hurtful assault by my mother, but I can recognize in her behavior, thanks to my expanded understanding of war trauma, an eruption of emotional, traumatic wartime experiences. It was as if an intrusion, an emotional flooding, caused my mother to lose her grip on reality.

What was it actually about? Today I know that my mother's father died in the Piotrków Ghetto. My grandfather Meylech could not be saved because of his sickly constitution, but above all because of his traditional Jewish appearance and because of his poor Polish language skills. He died in the ghetto because he could not, and did not want to, disguise who he was. One could also say this: He did not surrender his identity, not even to survive. Today I suspect that my mother had a much closer and much more intense relationship with her father than she ever could admit. That she could not save him must have caused her severe feelings of guilt. As the flipside of this coin, it seems fitting that at times she ventured to say that she regretted having saved her sister and mother. Furthermore, I ask myself what it may have meant for her that her own survival was only possible because she betrayed her Jewish identity, whereas her father had to die because he remained faithful to his identity. I think that these feelings of shame, guilt, and rage that she had "failed" her father resurfaced in her relationship with me, and she therefore lashed out at me so full of hatred when I did not want to let myself "be saved." Did she want—unconsciously—to make amends with me for what she could not accomplish for her father? Anyway, I reaped hatred with my refusal.

When, years later, after this unspeakable nightmare, I had seen through Stettbacher's system and confronted my mother with his fraudulent behavior, I triggered another war experience and became the victim of a further projection: the greatest fear of my mother during the war was to be discovered, exposed. I hit exactly upon this emotional sensitivity when I confronted her with the truth about Stettbacher: I exposed her. I unveiled a secret. I destroyed a part of her history as a successful researcher on childhood. Her old fears returned, and I became—unwittingly—a persecutor.

It is interesting how my mother reacted when I confronted her with the truth in 1994. In contrast to her usual manner, there was no outburst. In fact, she remained calm and composed. Because of my excitement I did not notice it. Only today, looking back, do I register this behavior. The survival mechanisms of my mother were reactivated. She had to find a way to shake me off as pursuer. The letter of 1998, as I see it today, fit in with her strategy. She pacified me and thus averted the greatest danger. Outwardly, she began to draw a veil of silence over me and to generally repress and deny the whole Stettbacher story.

The power of the never-processed war trauma was monstrous: in her eyes, I became the persecutor and blackmailer, a figure from World War II, and my mother forgot in her delusion that I was her son.

THE END 2009/2010

Why I reestablished contact in 2009 I have described in Chapter II. As said before, the estrangement could not really be overcome on my part. My mother wrote me, three days before her predetermined death, a letter for my 60th birthday which says, in a friendly tone, that she had made her peace with me: "What a pity that we could only now talk more freely with each other, but I am very glad and grateful for what you have been able to tell me during our last conversations, so openly, so truthfully." It is hard for me to let this stand. Her attacks against me during the 1980s and 1990s were so massive. Her pattern of comparing me to my father took on a different, more pernicious dimension after my research into her war experience, and my discoveries in this regard throw a different light on our difficult relationship. Today, I hear more and more in her reproaches that I resembled my father the echo of how she identified, in turn, my father with her Nazi blackmailer. In her attacks, she thus identified me with the pursuing Nazi. Even though she herself, in her repression of her war trauma, never established this direct connection.

During the research for this book, I also met the Berlin trauma therapist Oliver Schubbe. He visited my mother several times in the year 2000 in Saint Rémy to do therapeutic work with her. My mother released him after her death from the confidentiality obligation. In response to my question what had motivated her to once more undertake an attempt at therapy, Oliver Schubbe replied:

> Your mother contacted me because she was having strong physical pain all over her body; no one could find a physical cause. She wanted to find out why she had such pain. From her self-understanding, it was clear to her that the pain had to have a psychological background. For her it was clear: the body never forgets, the body stores memories that must be resolved in order for the pain to vanish. Very soon, your mother admitted still another intention of her self-discovery: she was suffering from great guilt feelings because her relationship with you was so difficult and burdensome. She finally wanted an authentic and honest, an easy relationship with you, free of conflicts. She described to me the anxieties she would have when she had contact with you. Whenever you would call or write to her, the pain would appear like an ambush for quite some time. On the one hand she had deep feelings of guilt towards you, on the other hand also rage and acute fear of pain. She was afraid of any contact with you and that you would emotionally and financially exploit her. The contacts with you reminded her of your father and the Nazis. In our therapeutic work she wanted to find out how this projection towards you was taking place.

Amazed I asked him if my mother had established a connection to her war experiences. He affirmed this. She had especially worked on her Warsaw war memories, which she had published in 1998 in her book *Paths of Life*, disguised in anonymous form in the chapter about Margot and Lilka. She had terminated her therapy with Schubbe after only two weeks, because the pain had diminished. Unfortunately, it had been far too brief a period of treatment to adequately address her grave experiences in wartime.

Here I return to Erwin Leiser's above-cited book *Life after Survival*. For me it is obvious, three years after her death, after decades of cluelessness, how strongly the unprocessed trauma was on display in my mother's everyday life. And not only in the context of the Stettbacher story. Her compulsion to control, once vital for her survival, her unrelenting fear of persecution, which expressed itself in her complete withdrawal into her Provençal fortress, provide eloquent testimony. The more my mother labored to escape the agonizing ghosts of the war, the more the past manifested itself as the living present. And during the final years of her life, this past was directed more and more against her own son. Erwin Leiser says about this:

> Those who have emotionally and physically come into contact with death are marked by this encounter. Often they don't realize that this experience stains later actions and reactions, fears and wishes … they all, as survivors, as the ones who escaped, have similar difficulties with a world in which they have to find their way. The break in the reality of the survivors, who live at the same time in two worlds, because the past penetrates into their present everyday life, is typical for the survivors of the Holocaust … their past has also an impact on the lives of their children. (Pages 21–22)

Meanwhile, the trauma therapist Katharina Drexler writes in her essay "Trangenerationally Passed-on Traumas and EMDR—A Case Vignette" (2005): "Unresolved traumas can be transferred onto the next generation to a grave extent. This we know at the latest since the examinations of children and grandchildren of Holocaust survivors. This transference onto the children happens by introjection of the traumatized parent."

IX. Tested Knowledge— The Therapist

Despite the disastrous experiences I had with my mother, I cannot emphasize enough that those experiences in no way diminish for me the importance of her work. I consider her first three books, the themes of which she continuously expanded and deepened, as groundbreaking. The fact that Alice Miller was not capable of living according to her own findings is a different matter. In this chapter, I therefore would like to outline what kind of experiences I have had using the ideas of my mother in my concrete practice of therapy. I want to clarify how far the psychotherapeutic ideas of Alice Miller have practical relevance. This clarification must take into account two insights of equal importance to me, although they may seem mutually contradictory:

1. The theories of my mother form the basis of my therapeutic work.
2. The ideas of my mother can only partially be implemented.

Unfortunately, I never had an opportunity to examine these questions with my mother. She herself never tested her theory in her own practice. After the break with psychoanalysis, she had essentially stopped working as a therapist.

THE CHANGE IN TIMES SINCE THE DRAMA OF THE GIFTED CHILD

When my mother published *The Drama of the Gifted Child* in 1979, the right of humans to their own selves, to their own originality, was of central interest. Social demands could be deduced from the insights of developmental psychology. This applied above all to the treatment of children. Parents were faced with brand-new behavioral requirements. For the first time, they were held responsible for their behavior in child rearing and its psychological consequences for the child. Most of them were at that time still conceptually involved in a system of child rearing that did not correspond with the new insights of science, nor the societal values coming out of the protest movement of 1968 in Germany. Caught up in "Poisonous Pedagogy," many parents were thoroughly lacking in sensitivity to their children's emotional needs. Alice Miller thus touched a sore spot: she recognized emotional suffering that was related to hurtful parental behavior. She had articulated, for the first time, the psychological impact of domination over children by their parents.

Over the years, society has increasingly recognized the value of the individual, and likewise has increasingly acknowledged the human need to develop psychologically. Every human being should have the right to develop his or her own potential. Every child is born with originality, and parents are tasked with nurturing and supporting their children in developing this originality. Concomitantly, it was only in this context that it became even conceivable to reproach parents for wrongdoing, for failing to support—or worse, for impeding—their children's growth as individuals.

Abuse, emotional and physical, mistreatment, and emotional torture through violence or heteronomy in child rearing could be identified and condemned. Parents who beat their children were pilloried.

The British psychologist Peter Fonagy describes in his book *Affect Regulation, Mentalization, and the Development of the Self* (2004) the development of a "false self" as "the colonization of the True Self." Parents, he postulates, exploit their children by occupying them with the parents' needs, much the way colonial rulers exploit their colonies. As a result, children no longer know who they are, and personality disturbances in their psyche develop which we deal with in psychotherapy.

Thirty years later, at the beginning of the 21st century, the right to originality no longer needs to be defended; nowadays it is mainly a question of if and how adult children can break away from the strangling grip of heteronomy. Today, every human being has to shape his or her life autonomously and individually. This means that detachment from the parents becomes, in terms of psychological development, a great emotional challenge. People who remain stuck in infantile dependency patterns derived from their parents cannot adapt socially.

Accordingly, the focus of psychotherapy has shifted decisively. In the past, it was simply enough to recognize that parental behavior had prevented one's own individual growth. But today, efforts focus on recognizing how maintaining a false self can threaten one's true potential. Only through actually breaking away from parental impositions and expectations can adults take control of their own lives.

Against this backdrop, how should my mother's theory be applied to modern psychotherapeutic practice? I begin with a criticism: the ideas, as my mother formulated them, are not workable in practice; in particular, her idea that one can treat oneself therapeutically without a therapist is an illusion. For therapy to succeed, a human counterpart is indispensable. Nor is her radical idea productive that adult clients hold their parents accountable for wrongdoing in child-rearing, that they spoil for a fight. This only creates further entanglements that do not lead to a resolution. In my experience, a productive course of therapy is one that helps clients process their own biographies in such a way that they are no longer blocked by life-hindering patterns learned in childhood.

Detachment from the parents also consists of recognizing and feeling that the adult no longer needs existentially and exclusively the love and attention of the now elderly parents. Adults can find other adults with whom to communicate emotionally, an option not available in childhood.

For my mother, however, the focus was increasingly on aggressive confrontation with the parents. This was informed by her own behavior: she could not refrain, again and again, from attacking her own parents. But it is never sufficient merely to identify one's own childhood traumas and get in touch with one's hurt feelings. In order to promote real progress, therapists must support their clients in discovering the world without fixation on their parents, and to live their lives autonomously.

KNOWLEDGE OF
ONE'S OWN BIOGRAPHY

Biography is primarily a history of relationship experiences. Biography is a mental synthesis of experiences with facts, emotions and the social environment—and the history one makes of it. Stored in the brain are one's experiences with other people, with oneself, and the impact one has had on others: our memories shape our biographies.

Whenever I help my patients reconstruct their biographies, I benefit greatly from one of my mother's prime concepts; namely that it is imperative to accept the child's perspective as genuine experience. This radically changes the therapeutic process and stands in stark contrast to other forms of therapy. Therapists acting as "enlightened witnesses" can forge new pathways for their clients: they are taken seriously in their perceptions and their experience. Supplemented by knowledge from developmental psychology, the therapist can also detect parental misconduct in the recollections of their clients, even from memories that, to the client, seem insignificant. The therapist has a sensitive ability to help detect "poisonous pedagogy" of parents' behavior in clients' childhoods. By confronting clients with this awareness, the therapist enables them to get a more nuanced sense of their lived biography. Through the process of tracking—that is, research of facts—one sets the groundwork for the client to experience pertinent feelings.

For a long time, I shared Alice Miller's belief that mainly repressed feelings are uncovered in therapy. Today I am no longer so sure. Certainly, it can happen that feelings are generated by a traumatic experience with one's parents, but those feelings are immediately repressed, rather than stifled by attempting to adapt. Having feelings at all was therefore prohibited. Brutal emotions of fear and aggression remain unconscious mental states, determined by biology. They only can become actual feelings through a transformation from biological, emotional experiences to mental sensations. Therefore, when clients, in the protected environment of the therapist's office, get in touch with pertinent feelings through the reconstruction of knowledge of their childhoods, it is an altogether different matter. Experiences that have previously been stored unconsciously in the body now connect for the first time with corresponding emotions, which then creates a markedly different mental quality.

Therapists support the development of the self, of self-confidence and self-assurance, when they help clients articulate their feelings about their parents. When clients notice their true feelings about their parents, and above all, process and understand those feelings, this is a clear response that cannot be surpassed.

Thus, the acquired knowledge of one's biography becomes a sort of inventory, a performance assessment of one's parents. Clients may claim the right to judge and evaluate parental behavior.

On the surface, this may seem perfectly benign, but even today this therapeutic process violates a social taboo. Such a critical appraisal of one's own parents is often met with any number of dismissive comments: "How can you be so hard on your parents? They did not know any better. They had such difficult lives. Parents only want the best for their children. Well, even though they did not know any better, they certainly did everything out of love. How can you be so ungrateful. ..." And so on.

But what happens if one "critically appraises" the way one has been raised as a child? Vehement feelings of rage, and even hatred, of mourning and of pain, but also powerful feelings of fear may all come to the surface. Above all, clients are confronted with the reality that they cannot change their history any longer, they cannot make up for anything, everything is in the past. No one can rid oneself of vehement, oppressive feelings through forgiveness or endless understanding. Nor can clients become children again and start their lives over. Neurotic attempts to unleash these feelings in order to shed them do not help either.

In my experience as a therapist, the raging inner child is only helped by the new perspective of offering oneself as an alternative to the parents, by becoming the mature caring adult for one's own inner child. Thanks to the acquired biographical knowledge, which shows what went wrong in childhood, clients learn for themselves to do things differently and better in the future. They can only make up for their parents' shortcomings by learning to treat themselves more caringly than they were treated by their parents. Neither is there anything to be gained in challenging one's elderly parents in the hope of rectifying as adults the damage suffered in childhood, nor in compensating for their childhood deficits with other people. Clients can rather learn to become a reliable partner for themselves, providing a supportive inner dialogue, thus ensuring that they can maintain their wellbeing autonomously.

❧   ❧   ❧

I owe to my mother's radical attitude the fact that I found the courage to implement this biographical analysis with my clients. She mercilessly denounced abusive parental behavior and could not be shaken out of her opinions by hurtful criticism. To this day, I have found no comparably radical a position in any other psychological work. My mother broke a taboo with her ideas. For this, one has to be grateful to her. Still today there are cultures that fundamentally reject any criticism of parents by their children. In all the world religions parents are sacrosanct, and their actions are given tremendous license. For many people, the quest for autonomy is a cultural impossibility.

It was not without reason that Alice Miller denounced religion and its repressive mechanisms in all her works, especially in the book *Thou Shalt Not Be Aware*. Here matters come full circle—as we now know—with her childhood. As a child, she already questioned her own religion, fought back against incomprehensible rules and rejected them. As an adult, religious systems remained for her comparable to paternal violence at a higher level. An almighty god became the perfect representation of paternal authority. In her criticism of destructive childrearing behavior, she reserved her strongest attacks for religious license; that is, she refused to accept religion as justification for parental actions.

To this very day, I continue to admire my mother's audacity in this area, her willingness to take everyone on. As a critic of society, she made a difference; as a psychotherapeutic approach, it is not advisable to invite clients to so fundamental a criticism of their parents. It is much better to help clients acquire the mental tools to develop a protective grown-up position towards themselves than to become embroiled for the rest of their lives in a fruitless dispute with their parents.

My mother would have certainly revised her radical stance if she had tried to validate her ideas in practice. She herself became a victim of her radical feelings of hatred for her parents. She never succeeded in escaping these feelings of hate.

MENTALIZING—A THEORY FOR ALICE MILLER'S METHOD

The scientific field of mentalizing is mainly the creation of developmental psychologist Peter Fonagy. In his book *Handbook of Mentalizing in Mental Health Practice* (2011) he describes how this mental ability is an essential factor of mental health. Especially in modern psychotherapy, independent of any psychological school, it is the main task of the therapist to empower clients to mentalize. If this ability, and the form of conversation based on it, are combined with the radicalism of Alice Miller, then therapeutic work becomes very efficient.

I want to summarize briefly the requirements in therapy according to Peter Fonagy: mentalizing means to notice mental states in oneself and in others. These mental states show implicitly or explicitly perceived reality. By mentalizing, I am able to recognize how I sense and experience the outer world in my inner mental world. Thus I can facilitate access to myself. The same is true in relation to others. Anyone who mentalizes can empathize with the emotional, mental world of somebody else.

By their mentalizing interventions, therapists open for clients their own mental world and that of others. The therapist is therefore an educator who pursues three goals: 1) To increase awareness of one's own and other's mental states; 2) To become aware that there are other perspectives, apart from one's own, of perceiving the world (the "theory of mind"); and 3) To regulate emotions. One can learn through mentalizing to modulate emotional states of arousal, and to feel emotions according to reality.

In general, mentalizing can be described as the capacity for reflection. One is able to think and cognitively process one's own psychic experience and that of others. Fonagy regards mental states as a highly differentiated mental spectrum, encompassing everything from daily needs, wishes, feelings, thoughts, beliefs, fantasies, and dreams, to panic attacks, hallucinations, or even all the way to delusions. Aside from the reflection of mental states, Fonagy attaches importance to the acquisition of competence in empathy and introspection. The process of introspection is the awareness of one's own inner mental life; empathy is understanding the feelings of others.

Therefore, it is of prime importance in the process of therapy to reconstruct one's biography factually and above all to experience it emotionally from the child's perspective. Until this has been accomplished, one is still trapped in the dependent childlike relationship with the parents, and still experiences childhood through the parents' eyes. The purpose of therapy is to disengage from this emotional bond with one's parents, and for oneself to become the contact person for the inner child. In therapy, clients mentally build a parent-child relationship with themselves.

In order to gain access to themselves, clients need to behave introspectively; if they want to understand, they need to empathize with themselves. This internal psychic structure, which has to be created anew, becomes the basis for acting in an adult and competent manner with the outside world.

Why does the child, even as an adult, shoulder the parents' viewpoints? It is here that mirror neurons come into play. Thanks to this biological neuronal structure, children internalize, by identifying with their primary caregivers, their earliest relationship experiences as a whole. The child feels and behaves as the parents do. Parental behavior towards the child settles in the self of the child virtually like a permanent resident, and later, in an adult who has not detached from the parents, exerts the same impact on their behavior and experience as in the past— no matter how far the adult has moved away from his parents' life plan.

Thanks to the consistent biographical analysis obtained in therapy, one is able to identify this repressed relationship with the parents. Thanks to mentalizing it becomes possible to get an objective view of the parent-child relationship. Hence one can learn to observe *and* feel, how we were afraid of our parents when we were children, how we adapted, what was done to us—everything is exposed, adults become eyewitnesses to their own childhood biographies. This process is accompanied by the most intense emotions. Here, the therapist helps clients to be protective towards the child they once were, and to argumentatively confront the parents within the framework of therapy. This dispute does not necessarily need to be argued with the elderly parents in reality; it may remain part of the therapeutic process. Yet, awareness of the parent-child relationship and the adults' conduct towards their parents undergo a profound change. Clients no longer remain in a position of the helpless child toward their parents, but enter into objective discussions as adults armed with the knowledge acquired in therapy; they meet their parents eye to eye.

My mother's error in reasoning is that she was convinced that as soon as clients were able to recognize their traumatic histories, they would be released from their mental suffering. Unfortunately, Alice Miller did not consider how endless disputes with one's parents can leave a client hopelessly enmeshed in stirred-up emotions. My own history with my mother bears eloquent witness to the power of this. When clients call their parents to account for their offenses, when they confront them with their "crimes," then they basically remain locked in their childlike position. When parents indeed have acted criminally, abusively or violently, against their children, it may be appropriate in such cases to bring them to justice. But as a rule, confrontations with parents about their childrearing misconduct are unproductive and do not bring about change for clients. The inner dialogue with parents leads much further.

My mother described very well in *The Drama of the Gifted Child* the pathogenic adaptation of the child to the expectations of the psychosocial environment. Clients can improve their relationship with themselves significantly when they learn, in role-playing for instance, to contradict parents as they had experienced them in the past. They can hold their parents accountable, ask questions that had always remained unanswered. As children, they did not have the slightest chance to understand what was happening to them.

It is interesting that clients usually know precisely how their parents would answer those never-asked questions. Therapy reactivates this knowledge. If clients are permitted, they automatically remember their experiences. It is often amazing how strongly they can identify with their parents. The therapist moderates this dialogue and in the course of therapy becomes indeed a true witness to the client's biography.

In such moments, I have often thought of my mother. She was right: clients feel protected by the therapeutic relationship. For the first time they can clearly articulate themselves autonomously as adults towards their parents. Clients learn to stand up for their hurt child.

This protective stance is another of my mother's concepts. It is particularly interesting how clients visibly relax as soon as they can logically, clearly, factually, argumentatively, and determinedly confront their parents. They no longer feel inferior, parents no longer appear superior, clients no longer feel powerless and helpless. On the contrary, they feel strong and equal.

Only after this process are many clients able to consider taking a new perspective towards their parents. They begin to understand, albeit not necessarily approve of, the actions of their parents. At this point, clients assume, as adults, responsibility for themselves. Clients become their own partner for their feelings, their needs, all their troubles. Finally they know how they can deal lovingly with themselves and their concerns. Only when they can be true to who they really are, do they have the possibility to live maturely in relationships.

THE ENLIGHTENED WITNESS—
THE RELATIONSHIP BETWEEN
THERAPIST AND CLIENT

Alice Miller introduced the concept of the enlightened witness into the discussion of psychotherapy. In childhood, such a human witness could have had the function of protecting the child from parental abuse, stopping parents in their destructive actions.

Naturally, my mother well understood that such an enlightened witness was more a wish than a reality. This is why she assigned the role of enlightened witness to the therapist in therapy work. She described the role of the enlightened witness as follows:

> Without the enlightened witness it is impossible to bear the truth of what happened to us in early infancy. But by the term "Enlightened Witness" I do not mean anyone who has studied psychology or has been through primal experiences with a guru and has remained in his thrall. For me, "Enlightened Witnesses" are therapists with the courage to face up to their own histories and to gain their autonomy in doing so, rather than seeking to offset their

own repressed feelings of ineffectuality by exerting power over their patients. (Article on Alice Miller's homepage, January 1, 2001)

Over the past decades, empirical psychotherapy research has also addressed the client-therapist relationship. Christoph Stucki for example convincingly described in 2011 the needs of clients in reference to the therapist: "I would like a therapist who admires me, who sees how I suffer, who allows me my freedom, who does not come too close, who never lets me down, who does not cause me pain."

Recent research broadens the role of the "Enlightened Witness" considerably, but unfortunately what is missing is an intrepid, radical view toward parental conduct in order to experience and process one's own biography. The researchers clearly highlight of course that disappointments and rejections in childhood lead to mental illness, but they avoid to call concretely by name the burdensome experiences of clients. The psychotherapy researcher Klaus Grawe (1943–2005) emphasized particularly in his research that humans have basic needs that absolutely must be fulfilled: attachment, self-worth, control, and the avoidance of displeasure and the pursuit of pleasure. All four are socially defined and their satisfaction creates well-being in humans that constitutes mental health. Humans depend existentially on social relationships. They need the freedom of action to feel they are socially included and able to elicit social resonance in others with their actions. This also implies that our actions have meaning. Furthermore, humans need self-affirmation. Feedback is existentially important. We all have the need to be validated and loved as our true selves.

In addition, the avoidance of displeasure and the pursuit of pleasure are essential: humans know from experience what they want and what they do not want. They develop a knowledge of their preferences and fight back when these are not respected.

According to Grawe, humans are further driven by two different motivational modes: on the one hand the approach mode, on the other hand the avoidance mode. Basic needs are satisfied by the approach mode. Unpleasant, harmful consequences of the environment are avoided. But when people have experienced in childhood that their basic needs were not fulfilled, causing negative feelings, they later defend against those needs by means of the avoidance mode. They want at all cost to avoid further disappointment. Yet basic needs cannot be repressed, and thus a state of stress results that can only be compensated for neurotically. Consequently, Grawe argues that therapists, in their way of shaping the relationship with their clients, should encourage them to fulfill their basic needs in the approach mode.

The therapeutic ideas of my mother and recent approaches in therapy diverge significantly. In my experience, therapeutic efforts can be successful when both approaches are combined: by developing an adult self, clients develop with the help of the therapist a kind of inner moderator who is able to satisfy basic needs. Adults stand up for themselves and learn, despite difficulties, to remain in the approach mode. They no longer immediately take refuge in the avoidance mode, as they did as children. They know exactly when approach or avoidance are called for. As adults, they can decide freely if they want to say yes or no.

The attitude, the behavior of the therapist, stands as a model. In a playful way, therapists assume the role of "Enlightened Witness" and take on motherly functions, as Christoph Stucki formulated. Clients store this experience as a sequence of action and draw on it if needed. Thus they internalize the therapeutic attitude towards them as an attitude towards themselves.

What Remains of The Drama of the Gifted Child?

At the beginning of this chapter I wrote that the work of my mother is the basis for my therapeutic work, although in practice one can apply her theories only with distinct limitations. I trust I have made clear why I think this is so. In any case, there are three elements of her thinking that remain today, and will remain in the future, important pillars of therapeutic practice: 1) The passion with which she stood up for the emotional interests of children, her ardor for the right of the development of the true self; 2) The invaluable significance of the therapist as enlightened witness; and 3) The transformative power of biography work. These three guidelines are indispensable in my work as a therapist, and I am convinced they will remain so. How wonderful it would have been had I been able to exchange views about all this with my mother, with Alice Miller.

My Mother's
Last Letter of
April 9, 2010

*M*y dear Martin,
  I wish you all the very best for your birthday, a beautiful party and that you feel good about all that you have accomplished in these 60 years.

 My death should not keep you from this joy because you know indeed that it will mean absolute salvation for me. No mother lives forever, eventually this farewell must happen. What a pity that we only now could talk more freely with each other, but I am very glad and grateful for what you have been able to tell me during our last conversations, so openly and so truthfully. I hope that the two of you will have many more beautiful years together and embrace you with all my heart,

your mummy

X. On Breaking the Wall of Silence—Afterword by Oliver Schubbe

"*There is not a crime, there is not a dodge, there is not a trick, there is not a swindle, there is not a vice which does not live by secrecy. Get these things out in the open, describe them, attack them, ridicule them in the press, and sooner or later public opinion will sweep them away. Publicity may not be the only thing that is needed, but it is the one thing without which all other agencies will fail,* " writes the journalist Joseph Pulitzer.

To keep injustice quiet protects the profiteers. The present generations of pensioners did not profit from World War II, but suffered for more than half a century from the war experiences of their childhood and youth. Parental behavior conveyed to Martin Miller and the postwar generation what war, flight, displacement or rape mean. Often this happened without words, without explanations, without frank discussion. In order to understand and process their experiences, both generations must overcome the separating wall of silence and courageously look behind the scenes of the past.

The encounter with Martin Miller, who visited me in Berlin while doing research for this book, was in this respect unique for me: never have I come to know a human being so full of respect for everything alive and for everything that is human, who at the same time tried so unsparingly to understand his history, who was so exactly and curiously interested in my awareness. It touched me deeply how seriously he struggled again and again for this understanding. In the same way I had experienced Alice Miller's seriousness twelve years earlier in her efforts to overcome her own childhood and war traumatisations on a physical level, and to open herself more in her relationship with her son.

Those who, like Alice Miller, were born between 1917 and 1945, did not participate in the election of Adolf Hitler, but experienced directly the horrors of war. Half of these "war children" experienced a traumatic event; one-third of them suffers from psychological post-traumatic stress; and one-fourth of these children is seriously limited because of this in the fulfillment of their lives. Symptoms like nightmares, overwhelming images of memories, psychosomatic health problems and pain occur for most people when strength declines with age. Psychic defenses decrease, and there is less and less physical energy to compensate for the feelings and physical states connected to war memories. Memory states become for some like an inner prison from which there is no escape. Others are pursued by chronic pain, or are helplessly at the mercy of their psychosomatic symptoms. Anxiety disorders, depression, and psychosomatic ailments occur significantly more often in this generation.

For a long time, people with such symptoms were left on their own. Among other things, there were simply actuarial reasons for this: the sole diagnosis for psychological consequences of war and violence had already by 1926 been struck off the Reichsversicherungsordnung (German Social Insurance Code) following World War I. This is why during World War II "traumatic neurosis" was neither identified nor treated. A new, trauma-related diagnosis was introduced again only in 1980: post-traumatic stress disorder. This gap in the insurance code had far-reaching consequences: what does not officially exist can not be treated in the healthcare system, nor can it be compensated or researched. In addition, psychological research devoted itself at first not to the general population, but to the most severely traumatized victims of the Holocaust, and later in the United States to veterans of the Vietnam War. Secondary trauma consequences were taken even less seriously and initially only studied in children of Holocaust victims, and after 1980 in children of Vietnam veterans. But many more people are affected by the consequences of war and persecution, flight and displacement, even though they are emotionally stable.

The post-war generation experienced the psychological consequences of war with their parents and the impact of war on society. Parents impart their emotions to their children by body posture, gestures, facial expression, the look in their eyes, voice, granted or denied touch, while they lacked the words to describe their feelings and to explain their origins. What was not spoken left the children alone with their questions: Why did they have to eat every morsel on their plates? Why were they not allowed to throw anything away? Why did their parents not give them hugs? What was so wrong with the rage of the child? Why were strong feelings not acceptable? Why did parents consider the worries of their children as matters of little importance? Why were they often not consoled? Why did parents not respond more strongly to their needs? Why were parents sometimes so unbalanced or overburdened? Why did they have to function as children for the benefit of the family and assume responsibility early on? What made these things so important—external security, room furnishings, toys, allowance, travels—in short, everything their parents had missed?

Many children of the war generation sensed these questions, but never could put these questions to their parents—as Martin Miller accepted as a boy the command for silence in his parental home. Like most children of his generation, he applied the behavior of his parents to himself, sensed early on their neediness and tried to make things easy for them, when possible to calm and comfort them. Only the fewest parents could allow closeness, bodily contact and intensity of emotion after the war. Parents expected their children to manage on their own the usual problems of childhood and puberty. Thus the principle of care was turned upside-down and children were robbed of a part of their childhood. Instead of recognizing this loss and mourning it adequately, they dedicated themselves to their work and families—and achieved the high value that prosperity and security had gained during the war.

During the fifties, war-torn Europe flourished. Even the GDR (East Germany) became economically the strongest state of the Warsaw Pact. Some turned their back on the past by making a new start and emigrating. However, behind the facades of the new orientations of society and politics, the post-war generation was clearly affected by war and national socialism. Fascist violence, traumas, fears, inferiority complexes and aggressions were largely passed on after the war outside of the eye of the public: within the family. Thus entanglements with national socialism, domestic violence and war experiences became taboo. For decades, many families repressed this chapter of their history. Family Miller was no exception.

It is extremely difficult for the succeeding generation to grasp the connections between World War II and their own lives. They no longer suffer from the typical symptoms of post-traumatic stress disorder but, for example, from constantly recurring blocks, diffuse anxieties, the feeling of being without home, guilt feelings heavy as lead, depressive moods and the deep uncertainty of not knowing the cause of their problems.

At the same time, the mechanisms of secondary traumatisations have by now been sufficiently researched to account for how they are passed on by learning experience, by bonding experience and direct biological transmission.

Modeling their parents, children learn also what is not spoken, such as the fear of particular situations, the importance of feelings such as guilt, the trivialization of their own problems, or the high value of being safe. Children learn to be overly watchful and fearful, and difficulties arise from this with detachment and individuation. They learn what they are allowed to talk about—and what is not allowed; when there is no room for questions and discussion, it does not matter whether parents spare their children horrible war stories, or tell them their war stories. Through the parents' model implicit messages are passed on to the children, and the attempt of the children to understand the agony of their parents, which they perceive, fills the black hole of silence with fantasies.

The capacity to bond is also affected by psychological traumatisations. It is then that children experience less empathic, less emotionally open and present parents, who in addition respond significantly less to their children's needs. The lack caused by traumatisations can have an impact decades later because the bonding experience has far-reaching consequences for the feeling of being at home in the world, for emotional equilibrium, for dealing with stress and the ability to form relationships.

Sensitivity to stress is passed on biologically. Research results up to now indicate that under the influence of traumatic stress the DNA molecules are directly affected; methyl groups are being changed like locks at certain base pairs. (This field is known as epigenetics.) Several studies show that children of traumatized parents share the parents' lowered level of cortisol, and exhibit post-traumatic stress syndrome more frequently than other children. The inheritance of a heightened susceptibility to stress through key genes has been detected in children as far removed as four generations. However, this susceptibility can indeed be influenced by proper nutrition and stress management.

Silence cements the violence that marks relationships and protects the perpetrators, rather than those who got away— the survivors who try to contain the flood of traumatic memories in silent horror. It only seems to protect the family when children and grandchildren show consideration for parental taboos. In reality, fear and silence concretize the societal conditions for war and violence and the questionable peace between victims and perpetrators. Fear and silence, like an invisible wall, block the psychological and societal reappraisal of what happened.

The path of reappraisal proceeds like a spiral over several stages. Every individual story weaves a new thread into the emerging fabric. Initially it is a matter of expressing and listening to personal truths. Then facts have to be documented, evaluated and publicly discussed. As a society, we have to assume responsibility for the reappraisal, we have to acknowledge the survivors—those who got away—and the damage suffered, and to once again enable our government to protect the basic rights of every human being.

The first phase of the Federal Republic of Germany from 1945 until 1960 was marked by making taboo and not addressing the Holocaust and war traumas. In East Germany, a comprehensive "denazification" took place, but there was no examination of the consequences of traumatic experiences. Contrary to expectation, even traumatized Jews met a wall of silence in their new homeland Israel. Only with the Eichmann trial in 1961 did a new phase of coming to terms with the past begin in the Federal Republic (West Germany). With the Auschwitz trial in Frankfurt 1964/1965, the Nazi era became increasingly subject to scientific and political interest.

By now public interest in the themes of the post-war generation has risen even further. The subject of the children and grandchildren of war has found its way into television films and the theatrical stage. The dying off of the perpetrator generation contributes to a decline of tabooing—also in a negative sense: while many pledged after the war to prevent a new war at all costs, Germany once again, in league with other E.U. states, is a central actor in the world arms market that supplies regimes and dictators, and wages war once again, which is now called a "stabilizing mission." In order to provide the traumatized returnees from Afghanistan with adequate support, there would need to be societal understanding of "modern war" and the extent of the consequences of related trauma.

Psychotraumatology has experienced an enormous upswing globally during the past thirty years. Even until 1996, post-traumatic stress disorders were considered extremely protracted and difficult to treat. The efficiency of trauma-oriented psychotherapy has increased significantly since then. Meanwhile, trauma-oriented psychotherapy is considered to be much more effective in the long run than treatment with psychiatric drugs. It remains largely unappreciated that symptoms arising from many years of war can be treated in a reasonable period of time, even in old age.

Aside from Lloyd deMause and Arno Gruen, Alice Miller was the founder of a new branch of scientific research: psychohistorical research addresses the unconscious roots of historical developments and societal norms, and these roots can often be found in childhood bonding experiences and psychic traumatizations. Psychohistorian Lloyd deMause describes as the decisive flaw of our historical development the reenactment of violence as a defense against dissociated psychic traumatizations. The wall of silence, and the reenactments of violence that take place behind it, lead to attachment disturbances in the individual, to violence in the family, and over and over again on the historical stage to war.

Alice Miller was a relentless admonisher of any kind of abuse of and violence towards children. With the adoption of the U.N. Convention on the Rights of the Child in 1989, all countries that have signed this convention—including the Federal Republic of Germany since 1992—have committed themselves to do everything in their power to protect children from all forms of physical or mental violence. On paper, children today are entitled to be raised without violence. Yet in 2011 almost half of more than a thousand German parents, interviewed by the Forsa Society for social research, had resorted to physical punishment, such as spanking and slaps in the face. About 14 percent even admitted to disciplining their children by means of painful beatings, or blows with a stick. Such bodily injuries are today in violation of existing law, but as a rule they still remain unpunished.

Alice Miller conveyed to her readers new hope to overcome the deadly cycle of war, attachment disturbance and domestic violence. In public she was the protagonist in the fight for self-realization and the protection of children; at home she was rather the protagonist of personal tragedy, repeating the cycle of attachment disorder and violence with her eyes open.

Alice Miller says in *The Drama of the Gifted Child* (first edition, 1981, *Prisoners of Childhood*): "Probably everyone has a more or less concealed inner chamber that he hides even from himself and in which the props of his childhood drama are to be found. These props may be his secret delusion, a secret perversion, or quite simply the unmastered aspects of his childhood suffering. The only ones who will certainly gain access to this hidden chamber are his children." Martin Miller not only had access, but also the courage to enter this hidden chamber. He investigates this chamber to its furthest corners, until he finally finds there the role he played, together with the props. The crucial point is that he does not stop at deconstructing the childhood drama of his mother. Instead he accepts his inheritance, fills the story with his own consciousness, and, becoming an author himself, rewrites it. Thereby he illustrates how the path of reappraisal for children and grandchildren can proceed.

Reappraisal is not a straight process, and assuredly not a rapid one. The readaptation to peacetime proceeds like a spiral over several generations. But if an Alice Miller did not succeed in breaking through the silence and the cycle of violence, will we, as parents, as society, then ever accomplish it?

Martin Miller has set out on his way. What is remarkable is that he has not remained alone on this path. He has looked for partners in this conversation, questioned contemporary witnesses, and taken himself mercilessly to task. His example gives courage. Could this widespread problem be solved only by team effort? Truth alone does not heal, but it is still a first step—and it is never too late for psychotherapeutic, familial and societal reappraisal.

Oliver Schubbe

www.traumatherapie.de
oliverschubbe@traumatherapie.de

XI—LETTER TO THE MOTHER

Dear Mother,

By now, my book about your life has already been on the market for four years and a lot has happened since then. At first I thought that after publication I would find tranquility in my relationship with my parents. But I was seriously mistaken. My book opened a Pandora's Box. From the reactions of the readers, and from people who knew you personally, I became aware that you had talked very badly about me behind my back, either repudiated or downright slandered me. Furthermore, I was faced with the question of why my father plays such a subsidiary role in the book. Book reviewers made me aware that my subjective experience and my person were not emphasized enough.

These criticisms and opinions were very thought-provoking for me. Now I have obtained from the publisher the rights of use for the English edition of my book, and I want to publish it in the United States. Based on the feedback I received, I decided it was imperative to add a final chapter for the American edition. With this in mind, I read my own book once again, and found myself growing irritated, especially by the book's opening. My book begins with a letter from you to me. It was the editor of the original German edition who persuaded me to begin my book off with one of your particularly dreadful letters to me, and even selected the specific letter out of my collection; I came to this painful realization upon re-reading your letter. This introduction had the effect of making the book less my own; your letter strongly influenced what followed. Today I deeply regret that I did not resist my editor's suggestion, which I realized was her subconscious effort to spare you. As a result, the objective criticism of my parents, especially of you, became diluted and weakened.

For the American edition of my book, I have decided to rectify my mistake; out of self-love I am taking this opportunity to respond to your letter.

In all honesty, I have to admit that I am only today able to reply to your letter, even though you have been dead for several years and cannot read the book nor my final letter to you. Until now, I did not possess enough knowledge nor the writing experience to stand up to your linguistic and intellectual eloquence.

You start your letter to me with the regret that I unfortunately did not accept your help. You claim that by making your offer to enable me to undergo therapy with the primal therapist Konrad Stettbacher, you had finally found a way to offset your failures as a mother during my childhood. But, alas, you came to the mistaken conclusion that I was so disturbed and confused that I had to reject your offer and refused to listen to you. Years later, you virtually blackmailed me into undergoing primal therapy. You did not respect my own viewpoint, even though by then I was more than forty years old. You resorted to the most heavy-handed tactics, threatening to use your considerable influence with the media to denounce me publicly as a charlatan. I agreed with a heavy heart, out of fear that I would lose the essential basis of my livelihood as a therapist. During this therapy with a student of Konrad Stettbacher, I virtually ended up in a cult-like group constellation. With my consent, the therapist tape-recorded my sessions, ostensibly as an aid to her method of treatment. Only by chance did I later learn that she had sent all of the tapes to Konrad Stettbacher. When I confronted her with my discovery, she said Stettbacher had received the tapes only in his capacity as her supervisor. In fact, Stettbacher passed the tapes of my sessions on to you—an egregious and unethical violation of therapist-patient confidentiality. You were thus able to monitor my therapy in real time. Regrettably, you never called this unethical conduct into question and never apologized for it. Despite feeling great fury and disappointment, I did not terminate the therapy because I lacked the courage. I became so desperate that I came close to throwing myself in front of a train and ending my life. But in 1994 I discovered that Konrad Stettbacher was not a legitimate therapist at all, but an impostor with a substantial share of criminal energy. His value to you, I realized, was that he was pliable enough so that you could use him to bring me under control. You nearly killed me.

Again and again, since this experience, I have racked my brain to figure out what would drive you to pit me against someone so hateful. Konrad Stettbacher literally persecuted me because he was rightly afraid that I would uncover his lies. Even during my first telephone call with him I had a queasy feeling that he lacked the competence required to be an effective psychotherapist. I informed you about this, and you became excessively upset. When I ultimately uncovered his malfeasance, I wanted him to have his day in court and be held criminally accountable. I was sadly disappointed again in that regard. Our Swiss justice system has no mechanism to criminalize deceptive business practices such as his. Thus, only a civil settlement was reached; Stettbacher was never criminally charged. I had to cope with the traumatic consequences of outright persecution on my own, and to this day, I have not completely processed what I endured. I am often reminded of it, and then I feel down. Hardest of all to forget is the feeling of helplessness when one is at the mercy of malicious people.

In your letter, you portray me as a virtual psychopath who denies his biography, is dominated by his father, and casts blame on you. You present yourself as a victim, and me, blind Martin, as your persecutor—someone controlled by his father, with a disregard for the truth. I know, however, that I am blameless in my actions toward you. I never acted destructively against you. I never gave you reason to behave so horribly toward me.

Now the time has finally come when I feel ready to confront you with the truth. Through conversations, and as a result of the consistent implementation of your own theory, I have succeeded in uncovering the mendacious secret of my family. Today I know that I became the victim of war experiences of you and my father Andreas. Thankfully I have such a good memory that I am able to remember exactly all my childhood experiences. I think this is only possible because those experiences were so bad that they burned themselves permanently into my memory. Your blunder of telling me that the Gestapo blackmailer during the war had the same name as my father put me on the right track.

I want to record in principle that you and my father lied to me throughout my entire life, and that I was born into your atrocious war relationship. There are compelling reasons why you never wanted to recount your war experience, and why my father cleverly avoided revealing himself to me in the slightest.

But as you have correctly described in your books, a person's history shows itself in the way that this person behaves toward his or her fellow humans. Likewise in your books you have stressed over and over again that parents act out their secret history, their repressed conflicts and disturbances, against their own children, thus behaving in a criminal manner. Since I not only helped you with the formulation of your books, but became the "enlightened witness," I was as much at home in your thoughts as a fish in water. Now I will confront you with your own suppressed history; only this will complete your biography and do justice to my book, which is incomplete in some respects because of the intervention of the German editor. I am holding you to your own precept that children should unsparingly uncover their biographical truth. With my letter to you, I satisfy your demand that all adults should reveal the truth about their childhood.

It is indeed curious how you always emphasize, in conversations and in your books, how essential it is for you that one uncovers and tells the truth. Your claim to truth runs through your letter to me as a persistent theme.

Imagine my shock when I discovered that my own parents had lied to me all their lives. Today I can see that when it came to keeping resolutely silent about your war experiences, you and my father joined hands as conspirators. In nearly all other respects, you were adversaries, constantly railing against and vilifying one another. Under these circumstances, I was unlikely to hit upon the idea that what most closely bound you together was your mutual war secret. You had to throw up a smokescreen to ensure that I would never see the secret you were hiding.

You only gave me a fragmented and selective account of your war experiences, as related in this book. But during the last four years I succeeded in uncovering the omissions in your war history and thus to finally and correctly sort out my suffering in the family. Now I will confront you with my true history:

When your whole family was deported to the ghetto of Piotrków, you very quickly became connected with the underground group in the ghetto and changed your identity. From one instant to the next you became another person. In place of the Jewess you became Alice Rostovska.

This is how you succeeded in fleeing from the ghetto; you moved to Warsaw where you earned money in the underground as a private instructor for Poles. In this way, you could also obtain false passports for your mother and your sister Irena and rescue them from the ghetto. Sadly you had to leave your sick father behind in the ghetto because, as an Orthodox Jew, he did not speak Polish but only Yiddish and would have faced certain death outside of the ghetto. Your beloved father died alone and abandoned in the ghetto. I am convinced today that your later rage at your father is an expression of the guilt feelings you had because you saved your unloved mother and abandoned your father.

Much later in your life, you dealt intensely with the sexual abuse of children. And yet, in your letter to me, while you allude to my beatings by my father, you devote not a single word to his sexual abuse of me, which hurts me profoundly to this very day.

For years, I had to wash myself every morning with my father, who observed and controlled me, and robbed me of any sphere of privacy. If I ever physically came too close to my father, for whatever reason, he accused me in a contemptuous tone of being "a fag." Every morning you were lying in bed in the adjoining bedroom, a silent witness to this abuse, and did nothing to protect me from this monster. For you to make the accusation, in your last will and testament letter, that I am persecuting you because I identify with my father, and to turn me in your letter into a Nazi—this is unbelievable and disconcerting.

When you came to Warsaw with your sister and mother, you had planned and prepared everything in great detail. You managed to hide them both in a Catholic convent. But you had to force them to give up their Jewish faith and be baptized Catholic. Your mother reproached you hideously for this, and badgered you until you gave in and began to look for a flat in the Aryan part of Warsaw. Yielding to your mother and searching for a flat outside of the ghetto was a suicide mission. You yielded for the sake of peace and responded to an advertisement for a flat. A handsome, tall young man answered. His name was Andreas Miller and he did not hesitate to exploit the situation. He turned out to be a Polish Gestapo blackmailer. He belonged to a selected group of better-off Poles who worked for the Gestapo and blackmailed Jews with downright mafia methods. If the Jews did not pay up or had the hopeless idea of resisting, they were handed over to the Nazis and shot at once or sent to the gas chamber in Treblinka.

You immediately understood that you had fallen into a dangerous trap, and you gave Andreas your last ring, a valuable piece of jewelry from your family treasure. Thanks to your intelligence and cool-headedness you realized as quick as a flash that you had only one chance to secure your survival—by seducing Andreas. You then fell in love with Andreas and you became a couple. The blackmailer was hooked, and for reasons of survival you had to cooperate with Andreas. Now you turned from victim into perpetrator. Together with Andreas, you most assuredly sent several Jews to their doom and thus have them on your conscience.

During the Warsaw uprising, you fled with your sister Irena to the Russian side, to the Red Army of Stalin. You told me that you cared for wounded soldiers in a field hospital. What is poignant about this story is that Stalin unexpectedly handed the Poles over to the Germans. He betrayed the Poles for tactical reasons in order to later build his Communist empire. Fatefully, for survival reasons, you first had to betray and abandon your father in the ghetto, then you betrayed together with Andreas your brothers and sisters of the Jewish faith, and in the end the Poles. After the war you went with your sister Irena to the university in Lodz. But unfortunately you did not reckon with your blackmailer Andreas Miller. He found you and came to the same university as you, and you became once again the couple you had been during the war. The fictionalized and deceitful story of my father was then enshrined in myth, to be told again and again: how you wanted to leave him at short notice thanks to your scholarship in Switzerland, and how he also managed, with difficulty, to get hold of a scholarship so he could travel with you to Switzerland. It has now become apparent through my research that my father flatly lied to me. It was not you who applied for a scholarship, but it was my father who organized everything, and you went along with him, like you did during the war. For me it is a fairytale that you were superior to my father. Since the war, you were dependent on Andreas all your life and never could separate. Your letter shows clearly how you could not get away from the Gestapo blackmailer. That in your hate-filled delusion you take me for my father and even turn me into your Gestapo blackmailer—this is a monstrous slander that has hurt me to the core.

How did this go on? After completing your studies in Basel, you and Andreas were married, and then naturally you had the need to start a family and thus became pregnant with me. But when I was born, the Nazi ideology of my father struck mercilessly. Suddenly Andreas was confronted with the absurd situation that he had fathered a Jew with you. He hated Jews and had persecuted them during the war. Now he was supposed to become a loving father of a Jewish son. As he did during the war, he exercised his violent control over you, and demanded that you give the child away immediately; thus you had to surrender me to the care of an unfamiliar acquaintance. His fathomless anti-Semitism incited him to such a degree that he accepted the possibility that his own son could die. This is how I came into the care of the acquaintance, and, as if by miracle, I was saved by Aunt Ala, Irenka's mother, and uncle Bunio, Ala's husband. All three of them were by chance invited for dinner by the acquaintance. It was then that Aunt Ala heard a baby's heart-rending cries. Startled, she asked what child was crying so much. The acquaintance answered icily: "This is the son of Alice." Instantly, Aunt Ala entered the room, took me into her arms, and without asking my mother she decided to take me home with her immediately. She and her daughter Irenka took care of me during the first seven months of my life. I heard later that you only very rarely came for a visit to Aunt Ala. But you never engaged with me, only spoke briefly with your aunt, and then left. My father never visited me at all. After seven months you took me home with you, but I did not do well at all and became very depressed.

For years, you served up the following story to me:

> Martin, I had to give you away because your father and I were writing our doctoral theses, and it was so cold in the room that it was unfavorable for you to stay with us. Further, you did not feed at my breast, you refused, and I was so overstrained. Unfortunately I then committed the greatest mistake of my life. When you were six months old, I had to travel to Poland because of my mother and left you behind at home. When I returned, you were depressed and the reason was that you felt abandoned by me. This is the reason why we never again found a way back to each other.

I was very shocked when I found out the real truth.

You state extensively your position on my father's beatings in your letter. Your guilt, because you never helped me and in particular never protected me from this brutal treatment by my father, saddens me still today. It especially grieved me when I saw in interviews how vehemently you took a stand against corporal punishment of children by their parents. I felt betrayed and deceived. When you defend your failure as a mother by arguing that you had not resolved your problem with your mother, you make the mistake that many people make. They always pass their culpability on to their own parents. Because you had such a bad childhood you could not protect me from this brutal Nazi; this is a denial of the facts. Since you survived the war because you cooperated with your blackmailer, it meant that you became complicit in other Jews being blackmailed and even killed. As a mother, you did not fight back for your child when I was born. Then you watched when my father, the Nazi, constantly beat and humiliated me. I can still remember very clearly how you silently sat alongside, your eyes filled with fear, hoping that he would not kill me. These shameful scenes are a mirror image of how you behaved during the war, when Andreas beat, humiliated, and tortured Jews. For you to accuse me in your letter of treating you as my father had treated me as a child is vile and dishonest.

This was my real situation at home, as I have described it to you: I became the Jew you persecuted, just as in Warsaw. I was excluded, and more so because you always spoke Polish with each other in front of me. At first I believed that you wanted to make a good Swiss out of me, but when I found out that Jews in Poland never spoke Polish but only Yiddish, I understood which role I had to take on—because Swiss German sounds similar to Yiddish. Even at home I became the victim of Polish anti-Semitism.

Only today am I able to tie up all the loose ends of my history. You always stuck together and used horrible violence against me so that I would never find out the real truth.

Now to the enigma of Konrad Stettbacher. When I as a therapist became autonomous from you, you could not stand my independence. I blossomed and came alive. It is for me a gruesome picture the way in which you, after the divorce from Andreas, internalized the blackmailer to such an extent that you became a perpetrator. The Jew was not supposed to live, he had to be persecuted as in the war. History was being repeated, in another guise.

Konrad Stettbacher took on the role of my father and the two of you once again made me the Jew. After I found out that Stettbacher was a simple seller of lamps and a criminal, you kept your relationship with Konrad Stettbacher secret from all other people, as you had done with the relationship with my father. You made me into a charlatan, you made me into a Nazi, and using primitive psychoanalytic babble you reproached me for my unprocessed problem with my father. Your claim that you are telling the truth is in itself an abysmally profound lie.

It is shocking to me how humans, out of pure misery and for survival reasons, can lose any moral compass and save their own skins at the expense of others—practically without feelings.

If one reviews your life, it reads as a chain of betrayals strung together. First you had to forsake your father, then you betrayed the Jews, then the Poles, and then above all your own child. And last of all you actively tried to kill your own son by identifying with your persecutor and by using Konrad Stettbacher as an instrument.

Thanks to the success of your books you created an Alice Miller who never existed in reality. You became the Alice Miller that you always wanted to be. In your books, you compensated for all the missed opportunities of your life. Many readers can identify themselves very strongly with this mother image that you ingeniously designed. Therein lies your great success.

In conclusion I want to address some favorable words to you. During my whole life I have never hated you, even to this day. Because I know that feelings of hate destroy a human being inwardly, and one never again gets the chance to live one's life.

Today I am confronted with the paradoxical situation that you harmed me, almost killed me—but thanks to your radical ideas I found a way to save my own life. I think that deep down, through your writing, you wanted to make amends, and I am so glad today that I have discerned the hidden message of a good mother inside you.

Sadly, you never had the opportunity to see how your own son put your own ideas into practice. Without your ideas I never could have become such a good therapist. Your ideas inform my work every day. But I can today accept your ideas in such a liberated way because I can also see and recognize you as the real Alice Miller, as the mother that I experienced in life—not the idealized mother.

In this spirit, I have become your intellectual heir after all and have not died.

With many warm regards,
your son Martin.

Acknowledgments

Only during the production of this book did I realize the risk I had undertaken in writing a biography of my mother. Even though I had read many biographies of children of well-known personalities, initially I cast all doubts about my project to the wind.

When children write about their parents, the results seem to fall into two distinct categories. Either the parents are over-idealized to the pain-threshold, or the authors lose control and express without restraint their hatred of their parents. Neither approach serves the reader.

At the outset of writing this book, I did not have much experience as an author. Evamaria Bohle, an editor at the Kreuz publishing house, gave me sound professional advice, and led me by the hand. She gave me the courage to face this challenge, and for this I want to sincerely thank her.

As described in the book, aside from drawing on my experiences with my mother and the emotions attached to those experiences, I set out to obtain facts about my mother's life. I knew very little about her life before and after the war. Therefore, I want to extend very warm thanks to my mother's cousins Irenka Taurek and Ala Damaz, for having so openly provided me with information, especially as this entailed some painful memories for them both.

Furthermore I want to thank the many people who encouraged me time and again to finish writing this book and not give up. I am especially grateful to my wife, Manuela Brechbühl Miller, who very closely confined and masterfully cushioned my emotional imponderables, and my friend Ruedi Schöbi, doctor of medicine, who participated with interest and empathy in the development of this book and stood by my side in countless discussions.

If one becomes involved with such a delicate project as this book, it is a stroke of luck to enjoy the support of a sympathetic listener. Barbara Rogers, a former staff member of my mother, accompanied my work both lovingly and patiently. When I had questions, I could always trustingly turn to her. For this, I would like to extend her the warmest thanks.

I owe a great debt of gratitude to the experienced trauma therapist Oliver Schubbe, who found the time, despite his heavy workload, to write such an enlightening afterword.

Finally, I want to thank all my friends who accompanied me emotionally and cheered me on while I was writing, and the many committed people in the Herder and Kreuz publishing house, who contributed to the success of this book.

Martin Miller

Abraham Dov Englard, grandfather of Alice Miller, lived with his wife Sarah during the beginning of the 20th century in Piotrków.

The extended Englard Family before 1923. In the back Gutta and Meylech (Alice's parents), Fishel with his daughter Eva and her mother; in the front Dora, Franja and Ala. (from right to left)

Gutta und Meylech Englard, the parents of Alice Miller

Alice and Andreas Miller during the 1950's.

Alice Miller – At the end of the 1970's.

Made in the USA
Las Vegas, NV
10 June 2022

50045714R00111